USING IMAGERY TO DEVELOP MEMORY:

A Guide To Memory Training Systems

by Michael T. Bagley, Ph.D.

Trillium Press
Monroe, New York

Copyright © 1987, Trillium Press, Inc.
All Rights Reserved

Trillium Press, Inc.
PO Box 209
Monroe NY 10950
(914) 783-2999

ISBN: 0-89824-0409
Printed in the United States of America

TABLE OF CONTENTS

1 INTRODUCTION 1
   What is Memory? 1
   A Brief History of Memory 2
   The Importance of Memory 2
   Why Is Imagery So Important To Memory Training Systems? .. 3
   Major Purposes of This Text 4
   Review of the Research 4

2 MEMORY TRAINING SYSTEMS 9
   Superlearning 11
   Learning Affirmations 16
   Psychoacoustics 19
   Relaxed Attention 22
   Mastery Skill & Performance Rehearsal (MSPR) 28
   Mental Screen 44
   Personal Information Processing System (PIPS) 46
   Keyword Method 52
   Link System 55
   Personal Triggering System (PTS) 57

3 INTRODUCTION TO MEMORY – IMAGERY EXERCISES 60
   Memory-Imagery Exercises: Terms & Concepts 60
   What Is Imagery? 62
   Major Image Components—ISM Model 62
   Types of Images 62
   How Are The Memory-Imagery Exercises Used? 63
   Suggestions For Using The Memory-Imagery Exercises 64
   Exercises 66

4 REFERENCES 110
   Bibliography: Appendix A 110
   New Age Music List: Appendix B 111
   Baroque Music List: Appendix C 112
   Research Studies on Imagery–Learning–Memory: Appendix D: .. 114

CHAPTER 1 INTRODUCTION

"All men can think because it is possible to put things before our eyes, the way those who invent trained memory techniques teach us to construct images."
Aristotle

What Is Memory?

Memory is defined as the "ability to remember; capacity to retain or recall that which is learned, experienced; what can be recalled to mind," *The World Book Dictionary*. The *Webster Dictionary* defines memory as "the act or power of remembering—all that one remembers."

All memory, whether trained or untrained, is based on association. It is the ability—consciously or subconsciously—to relate what needs to be remembered, to an event, situation, object, place, or person previously experienced. The process of successfully retrieving desired information from our mental library is memory. The basic memory rule is, "you can remember any new piece of information if it is associated with something you already know or remember" (Lorayne & Lucas 1974).

A Brief History of Memory

Researchers trace the origin of formal memory training systems to the Greeks and Romans. Orators from these cultures delivered lengthy speeches with unfailing accuracy because they learned the speeches, phrase for phrase, by applying memory systems. Their basic approach was to associate each segment of the speech with a familiar object, e.g., a painting, a piece of furniture, a tool, and/or with a familiar place, e.g., a certain room of their house, a tree, a garden, window, etc. Paivio (1971) credits Simonides (circa 500 B.C.) as having developed the first mnemonic system. "We should never have realized how great the power (of a trained memory)," wrote the philosopher Quintilian, "nor how divine it is, but for the fact that it is memory which has brought oratory to its present position of glory." (citation from *The Memory Book*, Lorayne & Lucas, 1974.)

In 1491, Peter of Ravenna wrote *The Phoenix*, which became the best known of all early memory-training books and brought the art of trained memory out into the lay world. In a book titled *Memory*, William Stokes, a philosopher and memory teacher of the late 1800's, emphasized the importance of memory when he said, "Let us hope that the day will come when it shall be considered as great a disgrace not to use memory systems as it is at present not to read."

The Importance of Memory

Memory is the concern of everyone. It is a process that involves the entire spectrum of learning and living. The mere fact that new information is accelerating at a much faster rate requires us to learn more, and learn it faster. Memory is the corner stone of learning. Virtually all learning is based on memory. Any student knows that the more s/he remembers, the better grades s/he will get from the teacher. To succeed in school one must learn the art of memorization. Every course, every subject demands students to memorize mountains of information, each day, each week. Developing good memory skills is the major "key" to high academic achievement. It is also crucial for achieving high scores on the SATs. Research indicates that the SAT scores are the single best predictor for success in college. The complexities of the business world are such that memory has become one of the most valued personal attributes of any business person.

A good memory can also lead to a more productive and successful life.

Why Is Imagery So Important To Memory Training Systems?

The pioneers in psychology—such as William James and Francis Galton—felt that imagery was a fundamental psychological aspect of the mind. Ahsen (1977) states, "if you are striving for a higher degree of personal excellence and achievement, you cannot experience the power of imagery without being changed, motivated and inspired to positive action. It represents a new science and practice based on the magic of image creation. One of the delights of mental life is the discovery of mental images. For they are among our most precious possessions. Imagery has become the lightning rod of human energy."

Perhaps the major breakthrough on the use of imagery in learning-memory was Paivio's (1971) construction of the dual-coding theory of memory. According to this construct incoming pictures and concrete words are assimilated via pictorial imagery and verbal coding concurrently. Today, numerous mnemonic techniques employ the use of imagery.

It is the image-making part of mind which makes the work of higher processes of thought possible. Hence the mind never thinks without some form of mental pictures. The thinking faculty of the mind thinks of its forms in pictures.

The image can scan material with amazing speed. Images can be manipulated and repeated—they can be highly interactive, vivid and powerful. Through imagery one can bring to mind an experience long forgotten. Imagery uses the whole psychological system. The image gives us pictures ... from the pictures (images) we receive somatic responses in the form of emotional feelings ... from the pictures and the emotional feelings come our thoughts and meanings.

Forming associations is the key to effective memorization—when these associations include "images"—"mental pictures"—the associations become rich, deeper and longer lasting. This fact has been substantiated in a number of research investigations. In the next section there are a number of studies presented that clearly demonstrate the effectiveness of using imagery for increasing memory and learning. In his excellent and extensive review of the literature, Kenneth Sheinen (1985) found that imagery is a viable and effective means for improving memory skills in children.

Major Purposes of This Text

1. To familiarize the reader with the nature and variety of memory training systems.
2. To demonstrate the effectiveness of using imagery for enhancing memory skills.
3. To provide the reader with many practical exercises for improving his or her memory skills.
4. To demonstrate how these memory training systems can increase one's rate of learning, level of productivity and self-image.
5. To encourage the wide scale use of memory training systems in our educational institutions, in our businesses, and in our homes.

Review of The Research

This section contains brief descriptions of thirteen studies which support the hypothesis that imagery has a significant effect on learning and memory. These studies are evidence that imagery has a positive impact as an instructional methodology.

A) Vander Veur, B. W.: 1975 (Reading)

Reported: Hypothesized that the more vivid images would be remembered better than less vivid ones. She devised imagibility rating (high, medium, low) for the 1,000 most frequently used words. She found that five-to-seven year olds learned and remembered high imagery words significantly more readily than low imagery words.

Vander Veur, B.W. (1975) Imagery ratings of 1,000 frequently used words. *Journal of Educational Psychology*, 67. 44-56.

B) Montague, W. E. & Carter, J. F.: 1973 (Reading)

Reported: Found that more vivid passages are retained more readily than less vivid ones and concluded that imagery serves as a mediator between verbal learning and memory.

Montague, W. E. & Carter, J. F. (1973) Vividness of imagery in recalling connected discourse. *Journal of Educational Psychology*, 64. 72-75.

C) Paivio, A. & Katz, A.: 1975 (Memory)

Reported: Using statistical measures and applying the dual-coding technique of associating a word with an image found that pictures are best remembered when transferred to one's own idiosyncratic mode of remembering.

Source: Paivio, A. & Katz, A. (1975) Imagery variables in concept identification. *Journal of Verbal Learning and Verbal Behavior*, 14. 284-293.

D) Lesgold, A., McCormick, C., Golinkoff, R.: 1975 (Reading Comprehension)

Reported: Found that without extensive imagery training, simply asking readers to "Image what they read" does not improve comprehension.

Lesgold, A., McMormick, C. & Golingkoff, R. (1975) Imagery training and children's prose learning. *Journal of Educational Psychology*, 67, 663-667.

E) Gambrill, L. B. & Koskinen, P.: 1982 (Reading Comprehension)

Reported: Found that imagery instruction prior to reading a text significantly increased scores on a comprehension posttest.

Source: Gambrill, L. B. & Koskinen, P. (1982) Mental imagery and reading comprehension of below average readers. Paper presented at the annual meeting of the American Educational Research Association, Mar. 1982.

F) Rose, M., Cundick, B., & Higbee, K.: 1983 (Reading Comprehension)

Reported: Found that verbal rehearsal and visual imagery increased comprehension. Posttests occurred immediately after reading and gains held up during testing one week later.

Rose, M., Cundick, B. & Higbee, K. (1983) Verbal rehearsal and visual memory: mnemonic aids for learning-disabled children. *Journal of Learning Disabilities* 16, 352-354.

G)   Bracken, B.: 1981 (Memory)

Reported: Found that college students could recall significantly more sentences when personalized information was included in the sentence.

Bracken, B. (1981) Relative imagery-evoking ability of personalized and non-personalized sentences. *Journal of Mental Imagery.* 5, 121-124.

H)   Pressley, M. G., Levin, J. R., Delaney, H.: 1982 (Memory)

Reported: Reviewed the Key Word method (which involves generating an interactive image of the word to be learned, e.g., to remember the Spanish word for "card" which is "carta" the student would visualize a shopping cart with a large card inside it) and found it to be effective in increasing memory of definitions, enhancing comprehension, and improving factual recall in science and social studies.

Pressley, M. G., Levin, J. R. & Delaney, H. (1982) The Mnemonic Keyword Method. *Review of Educational Research.* 52, 61-91.

I)   Pressly, M. G.: 1975 (Memory)

Reported: Conducted first controlled experiment aimed at determining if mental imagery can increase memory for written material. Pressly instructed eight year olds on progressively longer prose selections. They were then asked to read 17 segments of a story and construct a mental image for each. He found that this group (experimental) significantly out performed a control when asked to furnish short answers.

Pressley, M. G. (1975) Mental imagery helps eight year-olds remember what they read. *Journal of Educational Psychology.* 68, 355-359.

J)   Pressley, M. G.: 1975 (Memory)

Reported: Investigated the relationship between mnemonics and children's learning and found that children learn pictures faster than words, and that pairing the verbal and visual assists in learning paired associates, remembering pictures, and story recall. He concluded that instruction on how to develop pictures in one's "mind" is crucial.

Pressley, M.G. (1975) Mental imagery helps eight year olds remember what they read. *Journal of Educational Psychology.* 68, 355-359.

K)   Higbee, K. L.: 1979 (Memory)

Reported: Found that imposed pictures are learned better than words at any age, children become more mnemonic with age, and by ages six or seven children can produce internal elaborations for paired associates.

Higbee, K. L. (1979) Recent research on visual mnemonics: Historical roots and educational fruits. *Review of Educational Research* 49, 611-629.

L)   Radaker, L. D.: 1963 (Spelling)

Reported: Taught fourth graders to image a word on a blank screen and try to hold that image for up to sixty seconds. He found that with either two or six training sessions the experimental group retained correct spelling significantly more accurately than a control group. The effect held true at a one year retest.

Radaker, L. D. (1963) The effect of visual imagery on spelling performance. *Journal of Educational Research,* 56, 370-372.

M) Goodwin, N.: 1983 (Creative Writing)

Reported: Found that using imagery prior to writing activities increased students' abilities to produce vivid and creative prose.

Goodwin, N. (1983) Dancing in the stage in your head. *English Journal*, 43-45.

N) Gambrell L. B.: 1982 (Writing)

Reported: Found that by visualizing after a selection third graders produced significantly longer written passages regarding that reading selection.

Gambrell, L. B. (1982) Mental imagery and reading comprehension of below average readers: Paper presented at the annual meeting of the American Educational Research Assoc., March 1982.

CHAPTER 2
MEMORY TRAINING SYSTEMS

"Let us hope that the day will come when it shall be considered as great a disgrace not to use memory systems as it is at present not to read."
>William Stokes
>MEMORY, 1888

The basic aim of this Chapter is to provide the reader with a variety of memory training systems that can be used to improve students' memory skills. There are descriptions and exercises for each of the ten systems presented in this section. Some of the systems are comprehensive, while others are less complex. In total, however, the systems incorporate most of the current theories and practices on accelerated learning and memory. To refer to these systems as techniques or strategies would be unjust, as they represent a way of thinking. For some students the systems will represent a major shift in how one thinks and processes information. These students will need time to digest the philosophical and theoretical issues involved in these learning processes. The memory training systems should be looked at in terms of their interrelatedness. The important qualities of each system should be learned and synthesized into a whole, and from this whole should come a "conceptual framework" and "mind set" that can provide the learner with a new positive attitude toward his/her potential for learning. The systems must be carefully introduced. They should not be presented superficially nor rushed in their use and practice. They are not little gimicky devices, but rather, intricate processes of human functioning. Build success experiences in using the systems. Decide which system would be best to introduce first. Experiment with each of the systems. Make them fit your learning style and the learning styles of your students.

Here are the ten Memory Training Systems:

1 Superlearning
2 Learning Affirmations
3 Psychoacoustics
4 Relaxed Attention
5 Mastery Skill & Performance Rehearsal
6 Mental Screen
7 Personalized Information Processing System (PIPS)
8 Keyword Method
9 Link System
10 Personalized Triggering System (PTS)

MEMORY TRAINING SYSTEM 1:
SUPERLEARNING

DESCRIPTION:
The Superlearning Method consists of four major components:
A) desuggestionizing,
B) mind and body relaxation,
C) Baroque Music (with a tempo of 60-70 beats per minute) and,
D) presentation of spoken data (data spoken at 8 and 12 second cycles).

The method was first developed by Dr. Georgi Lozanov, a Bulgarian scientist who spent years researching accelerating learning. He found that by putting the mind in a certain state of relaxed alertness, there is no limit to how much or how quickly knowledge can be absorbed. Dr. Lozanov, who left the medical profession because of an intense passion for studying the theories of learning, speculated if you could have painless surgery, and painless childbirth, why couldn't you also have the painless birth of knowledge.

The first component which is desuggestion is what Lozanov calls the process of trying to overcome your pre-conceived ideas about the limitations of your mental abilities. He designed a training system to get individuals thinking that they can achieve much more than they have ever realized. It's a "positive" brain-washing to get people excited about their potential for thinking and learning. Following the "psyching-up" sessions, Dr. Lozanov taught individuals several traditional relaxation techniques, e.g., diaphragmatic breathing, progressive relaxation, guided imagery. These techniques produced a mind synchronization that significantly enhanced a person's ability to focus and concentrate. He believed that the brain, freed from all distractions that hamper its functioning, resembles a sponge able to absorb knowledge and information more accurately and more effortlessly. "With a slower heartbeat, mind efficiency takes a great leap forward." Next comes the introduction of rhythm (sixty beats a minute) of Baroque music providing an incredible "sonic massage" which helps eliminate the stress of hard mental work. Music history has it that Bach created much of his music to appeal to the mentality. This special Baroque music has a very slow base, beating like a slow human pulse. As you listen, your body listens too, and tends to follow the beat. There is a Baroque music list in the appendix section of this text. The final part of the Superlearning Method is the presentation of spoken data. Through extensive research Lozanov found that information spoken at cycles of eight and twelve seconds greatly enhanced one's rate and capacity of learning. Think of the eight second cycle as two bars of four beats or two frames of four seconds each. Each beat is one second. 1 2 3 4 / 1 2 3 4. During the first four beats you exhale and then inhale. The second four beats you hold your breath and listen to the data being spoken. You repeat the same sequence over and over. The pause between data bytes gives the brain cells a chance to rest a moment so that they are better able to register the next item. Each of these four major components is of critical importance to the success of the Superlearning method. Although this four-part system appears uncomplicated, it is, however, more complex and demanding than you might think. In the next section there will be specific objectives and activities to help you become competent in learning this special system for enhancing memory skills.

OBJECTIVE 1:
To develop several positive learning affirmations to be used during a relaxed state of mind

ACTIVITIES:
A) Discuss the nature of positive affirmations.
B) Make a list of positive affirmations.
C) Select one or more positive affirmations and silently repeat to yourself with meaning four or five times.
D) Use your positive affirmations while listening to Baroque music or during a relaxation exercise.

For more information on positive learning affirmations see Memory Training System # 2.

Example Positive Learning Affirmations:
I can learn anything.
My mind is super.
Learning and remembering are easy for me.
I am confident and relaxed.

OBJECTIVE 2:
To learn how to breathe in rhythm.

ACTIVITIES:
A) Practice making your breathing rhythmic. Inhale to a silent count of 4; hold to a count of 4; exhale to a count of 4; Repeat four cadences of this rhythmic pattern.

B) Practice extending the inhalation and the exhalation. Inhale using a count of 8. Hold to a count of 8. Exhale to a count of 8. Repeat this cadence several times.

C) Drop the silent counting and concentrate on the flow of air going in and out of the nostrils. Continue with a rhythmic pattern of 4, 8 or 12 seconds.

NOTE: Breathing exercises should always be done prior to Superlearning activities. This will help slow down body/mind rhythms to their most efficient levels. If your students are having difficulty with the breathing patterns use the following Guided Relaxation Exercise.

GUIDED RELAXATION EXERCISE: RHYTHMIC BREATHING
— Find a comfortable position ... and relax ...
— Let all your thoughts ... go ...
— Clear your mind ...
— Take a deep breath and slowly exhale ...
— Focus your attention on your slow and even breathing.
— Feel the relaxation ...
— Alright ... I want you to follow this breathing pattern.
— Inhale to a count of four ... hold you breath to a count of four ... exhale to a count of four ...
— Begin ... P[ause]* = 15 sec.
— Repeat four cadences of this rhythmic pattern ... count silently ... P = 60 sec.
— Alright ... now let us extend the pattern to a count of eight ... again do four repetitions ... P — 2 mins.
— Now I want you to focus your attention only on the feeling ... of the air flowing in and out of your nostrils. P = 30 sec.
— Your breathing is now in a smooth rhythmic pattern ...

* P = PAUSE (teacher remains silent during pause)

— You feel calm and comfortable ... and deeply relaxed ...
— Bring your awareness ... now ... back to your original setting.
— Slowly let your attention come back to your room ...
— When I count to five you will be back and alert ...
— One-two-three-four-five

* P = PAUSE (teacher remains silent during pause)

OBJECTIVE 3:
To learn how to concentrate on material being delivered in rhythmic patterns with and without music.

ACTIVITIES:
A) WITHOUT MUSIC—silently read the material as a voice recites it rhythmically. Breathe in rhythm on the eight beat cycle. Exhale/Inhale 1 2 3 4. Hold breath 1 2 3 4 (and listen to data).
B) WITH MUSIC—Close your eyes and listen to data being spoken. You'll hear the teaching for four seconds, then cite the information during the next four seconds. Breathe along the recitation—breathing out and in during silence and holding you breath as the information is spoken.

NOTE: Begin with 20 to 30 data units. Later you may wish to use 50 to 75 data units in one session.

INTONATION

Researchers have found that to keep the mind interested, it helps to vary the tone of your voice as you go through cycles of information. They recommend three tones of voice: normal speaking voice, soft whispering voice, and loud commanding voice.

For example:

		Voice Tone
1 2 3 4	1 2 3 4	
Silence	$2 \times 5 = 10$	Normal
Silence	$2 \times 6 = 12$	Soft
Silence	$2 \times 7 = 14$	Loud

Suggestions for making Superlearning work:
A) Thoroughly discuss the importance of having a positive attitude about one's ability to learn and memorize new information.
B) Make sure each student has several positive learning affirmations and that these short phrases are silently expressed during states of mind/body relaxation.
C) Expose students to a variety of Baroque selections. Have them breathe to the rhythm of the music.
D) Practice rhythmic breathing often and especially prior to a Superlearning exercise.
E) Begin by reading the data units as they are spoken by another voice in rhythmic patterns.
F) Use a limited number of data units during your initial experience with Superlearning.
G) Experiment with different cycle patterns, e.g., use two frames of six seconds each. 1 2 3 4 5 6 / 1 2 3 4 5 6
H) Go slowly with the process . . . relaxation is a skill . . . rhythmic breathing is a skill . . . concentration is a skill . . . we need time in developing skills.

For more detailed information read *Superlearning* by S. Ostrander and L. Schroeder.

MEMORY TRAINING SYSTEM 2:
LEARNING AFFIRMATIONS

DESCRIPTION:
Affirmations are one of the most important elements of learning and memorization. To affirm means to "make firm." An affirmation is a strong, positive statement that something is already so. It is a way of "making firm" that which you are thinking and imagining. Most of us are aware of the fact that we have a nearly continuous inner "dialogue" going on in our minds. The mind is busy "talking" to itself, keeping up an endless commentary about life, the world, our abilities, our desires, our problems, and other people. The words, ideas, images that run through our minds are very important. We act, or fail to act, not entirely because of "will" as is so commonly believed, but also because of imagination. A human being acts and performs in accordance with what he imagines to be true about himself and his environment.

Champions radiate confidence. Winners possess that magnetic energy that can almost be felt. Winners image what they want to happen—losers see failure. "Man surrounds himself with the image of himself." The image that we carry around about ourselves each day, directly affects our emotional and physical system. The thoughts we create and subsequently hold about a future event or situation can determine our level of emotion when the time comes to engage in that particular event. Our thoughts and images can lead us to a heightened level of enthusiasm or can seriously depress our whole system.

"You can if you think you can and if you think straight," says Dr. Norman Vincent Peale. "You can, if you exercise will and persistence and mental calmness, think your way through anything. Our daily existence . . . our success . . . our happiness . . . our future . . . are determined in the mind. The mind is where we understand, where we dream, and where we think."

It is this positive approach to mind and potential that young learners need to understand, believe in, and practice. Developing a positive attitude and a strong self-image is crucial to the success one experiences in learning and in living. Positive affirmations about oneself can have a major influence on the outcome of any situation. Therefore, if one thinks and believes that s/he can learn something new or remember anything, it is likely to happen. Learning affirmations are important tools for success. We need to have them and we need to use them on a regular basis. We need to personalize them and make them part of our existence. It should be the absolute primary goal of every teacher, trainer, leader, to get individuals to think more positively about themselves and their natural abilities and potentials. A great first step is to get people turned on to "affirmations." Here are a few just to give you some ideas:

"I have a great memory."
"I can do it."
"I can learn anything."
"My mind moves efficiently and effectively."
"I enjoy achieving my goals."
"Learning and remembering are easy for me."
"I always remember names."
"When I concentrate, I'm awesome."
"I have a great mind."
"I believe in myself."
"I can if I think I can."
"I never forget anything."
"My memory is my greatest asset."
"I am going to and I will."

Affirmations can be done silently, spoken aloud, written down, or even sung or chanted. A few minutes a day can make a big difference and will counterbalance years of old mental habits.

An affirmation can be any positive statement. It can be general or very specific.

In her exciting book, *Creative Visualization*, Shakti Gawain lists some important things to remember about affirmations. They are:

1. Always phrase affirmations in the present tense, not in the future. It's important to create it as if it already exists.
2. Always phrase affirmations in the most positive way that you can. Affirm what you do want, not what you don't want.
3. In general, the shorter and simpler the affirmation the more effective. An affirmation should be a clear statement that conveys a strong feeling; the more feeling it conveys, the stronger the impression it makes on your mind.
4. Always choose affirmations that feel totally right for you. What works for one person may not work at all for another.
5. Always remember when doing affirmations that you are creating something new and fresh.
6. When using affirmations, try as much as possible to create a feeling of belief.

Affirmations can be used alone or in combination with the memory **exercises** presented in the text. Developing and using affirmations is a very important strategy for enhancing memory skills.

MEMORY TRAINING SYSTEM 3:
PSYCHOACOUSTICS

DESCRIPTION:
Not only breathing patterns alter states of consciousness, but music has been found to change brain-wave activity. Tokyo researcher Dr. Norio Owaki did a ten-year study on the certain kinds of sound patterns that can induce alpha (calming) brainwaves. Dr. Lozanov studied in his lab music Bach wrote for Count Kayserling, "The Goldberg Variations," and found that, in particular, the aria with which it starts and ends could induce a meditative state with many beneficial physical effects derived from its slowing down of body processes. Pieces by other composers of the sixteenth to eighteenth centuries, written in the same musical tradition, were found to have similar effects (Ostrander & Schroeder, 1979). Lozanov and colleagues found that with this music the body relaxed and the mind became alert. This Baroque music has a very slow bass, beating like a slow human pulse. A good exercise is to monitor your pulse as you concentrate on this special Baroque music. It is extremely effective for appreciating the relaxing effect induced by this music. As you listen, your body tends to follow the beat. Your body relaxes and your mind becomes alert in the most simple forms of relaxation.

The use of Baroque music in Superlearning is to give you a "sonic massage"—to eliminate the stress of hard mental work. The music helps fix the focus of attention inwardly instead of outwardly. In addition to the slow movement of the Baroque music, there is another type of music that has been found to produce similar effects on the mind and body. It is called "New Age Music." *The Los Angeles Times* has been reporting on it regularly since 1982. Several books are now available and the number of album releases continues to soar. Many radio stations across the country are devoting at least a portion of their programming day to this sound. New Age music can best be described as gentle, flowing, sustained-environment music without tension or resolve. It is music that has been scientifically proven to produce dramatic changes in consciousness and to be ideal for relaxation and mental work. The music incorporates a multitude of sounds: synthesizer, chimes, flute, harp, bells, running water, birds singing, crickets, ocean waves, etc. It combines and blends these sounds into a very artistic pattern of music. What are the effects of New Age Music?

1. It produces a feeling of "positive emotions."
2. It stimulates the production of images.
3. It enhances the level of concentration.
4. It invigorates the imagination.
5. It can reduce tension as it has a soothing effect on your autonomic nervous system.
6. It produces a state of relaxation easier and more quickly.
7. It can re-energize the body and mind.

In the reference section of this text, you will find a list of New Age music.

"Music is a marvelous and extremely powerful tool," says Nancy Hunt, a St. Louis music therapist who works in a child-birth center. "Music [the Baroque and New Age type] has a direct physiological effect on people. It increases blood volume, decreases and helps stabilize the heart rate, lowers blood pressure. Perhaps the biggest part of music's magic is that it can transform an environment by changing our own state of mind." A 57 minute University of Massachusetts Medical Center television program takes its viewers through what is called "mindfulness meditation." The tape teaches people to pay attention to their body, the quality of their breathing, the sensations in their body, the music, and their thoughts as the thoughts move through their minds.

Dr. Jon Zinn—Director of the hospital's stress-reduction and relaxation unit—uses harp music as background for his tape program because he says, "The harp has traditionally been an instrument for healing and calming the mind."

In the last five years, the medical use of music has grown steadily, often in conjunction with other alternative non-medical practices like progressive relaxation, guided imagery, bio-feedback, etc.

Just how music works its wonders is something researchers are only beginning to understand. Both its physical and psychological responses involve complex brain chemistry changes, not only in the thinking part of our brain, but in our "emotional" brain, the limbic system, and the "primitive" brain, the brain stem, which controls heart-beat, respiration, and muscle tension. One theory is that some kinds of music can produce in the brain the same "feel good" chemicals that running and meditation produce. These are called endorphins, natural opiates secreted by the hypothalamus, which can reduce the intensity with which we feel pain.

Dr. Steve Halpern, a California composer and music-therapy researcher, says, "A personal library of New Age music can enhance your environment and your health. Music is energy, just like food. Having the right music around the house is as important as having the right food and the right vitamins."

The Baroque music with the special 60-70 beats per minute is most effective for the Superlearning memory exercises. The New Age music is recommended for using with most of the guided and non-guided imagery exercises found in Chapter 3.

MEMORY TRAINING SYSTEM 4:
RELAXED ATTENTION

DESCRIPTION:
The ability to relax attentively is especially important to learning and memory. The first tenet of skill in any field is relaxation: the skilled always "make it seem easy." The second tenet is complete attention: expert practitioners invariably "give their all." Indeed, relaxation and attention are mutually supportive. By relaxing irrelevant tension, the individual releases full energy and attention to the task at hand. Watch any great performance—a beautiful backhand in tennis, a perfect high jump, a magnificent dive, a great piano solo, and you will see perfect harmony of mind and body. The importance of relaxed attention "focus" is particularly critical in thinking and learning, man's highest form of humaness. "We think and learn with our entire body, our whole being," says Robert McKim (1972). According to psychologist, Dr. Bruce Baldwin (1985), stress and your thoughts (cognitive processes) are intimately related. He states, "Tension and stress directly affect our cognitive abilities, including memory, in five major ways," which he refers to as "cognitive stress symptoms." They are:

a) short-term memory,
b) ability to store information,
c) attention span,
d) concentration, and
e) attitude.

He suggests, "Overly tense muscles direct attention, restrict circulation of blood, waste energy, and stress the nervous system: uptight body, uptight mind." "Memory works best, it would seem, when the mind is free of stress and is in a state of dynamic relaxation" (McKim, 1972).

Relaxed attention occurs when the relative balance of relaxation and tension brought to a task is appropriate. Bernard Gunther (1968), in *Sense Relaxation*, calls this relevant balance "optimal tonus." Edmund Jacobsen (1957), in *You Must Relax*, calls it "differential relaxation." Both concepts describe the human mind adjusting dynamically and economically to the task at hand, never pushing, straining or wasting unnecessary energy. Dr. Barbara Brown in *New Mind, New Body* says, "With a slower heartbeat, mind efficiency takes a great leap forward."

When balance or harmony of mind and body is achieved, we can say that there is a "mind synchronization." "Mind-synch" will be a term that I will use throughout this book. It will refer to a state of mind readiness achieved prior to engaging in a memory exercise. When we attain this focused energy state, new data can be processed and memorized effortlessly and efficiently.

In Chapter 3 there are twenty-one memory exercises using the tool of "Mental Imagery." The activities are designed so that students will reach the mind-synch level before engaging in the specific exercise. These focusing-of-the-mind exercises allow students to shift from Beta consciousness to Alpha consciousness.

In this next section I will discuss the effects of processing new information in an Alpha state of consciousness.

HOW DOES A SHIFT IN CONSCIOUSNESS AFFECT THE PROCESSING OF NEW INFORMATION?

An increase in the ability to concentrate is generally accepted as one of the most important variables affecting the information processing system. Another theory relates to the physiological changes caused by altered brain wave patterns that might be produced through a relaxation and/or a guided image experience.

Physical chemist Ilya Prigogine recently proposed a theory that earned him a Nobel prize. The theory—already confirmed by experiments—is called "the theory of dissipative structures." Brain energy is measured as brain-wave levels on an EEG machine. The up-and-down patterns of brain-wave levels reflect a fluctuation of energy to the brain. In full, normal Beta consciousness, brain-wave levels show up on an EEG graph as small, rapid, up-and-down lines. There is little fluctuation in the level of energy. However, in an altered state of consciousness through relaxation or imagery, brain-wave levels shift to alpha and theta. In these altered states there is a lot of fluctuation in the level of energy. According to Prigogine's theory, small fluctuations of energy (such as beta rhythms) are suppressed by the brain so it stays essentially the same. That's why changes suggested to a Beta conscious mind usually have little effect. The message is suppressed by all the existing programming. However, Prigogine says, "large fluctuations of energy (such as alpha and theta rhythms) can cause the structure to break apart and reorganize itself into a more complex and higher form. That's why suggestions or images given to an individual exploring in Alpha brain-wave levels are so effective in creating change. The new suggestion, dropped into the uneven Alpha rhythms, is like a pebble in a pond. It creates a ripple effect that tears apart old programming and creates new behavior and viewpoints."

Alpha and Theta brain-wave levels create large fluctuations of energy through the brain. Brain researchers claim that information going into an Alpha mind has 50 to 100 times the impact that information going into a Beta mind has. More research is needed in the educational environment in order to understand the significance of this claim.

Relaxed attention can lead to "Mind Synch," which can lead to a shift in brain energy. A shift or lowering of brain energy can lead to increased learning efficiency. Increased learning efficiency can lead to improved memorization skills.

NOTE: While a shifting of consciousness, brain-wave energy, has been scientifically proven to enhance memory it would be **inappropriate** to think that a prerequisite to **all** thinking and learning is altered brain-wave patterns.

Educators must use the mind tools of imagery in an effective balanced manner. Too much of anything is no good, e.g., the educational system over uses analytical and logical processes. Students spend approximately 95-98% of their time thinking and learning in Beta consciousness and 2-5% of their school time in Alpha-learning. I am recommending that we increase the Alpha-learning experiences to a ratio of 80% Beta to 20% Alpha. Although this ratio is statistically imbalanced, it is appropriate for productivity and success in school and in life.

Research has reported that most of society's so-called "Peak Performers" spend a great deal of time functioning in Alpha states of mind (problem solving, memorizing, decision-making, strategic planning, etc.) (Garfield, 1984). Their use of mental imagery processes in their basic lifestyles should tell us something of the importance of this human characteristic. Healthy people use more Alpha.

HOW CAN RELAXED ATTENTION BE ATTAINED IN THE CLASSROOM?

There are numerous ways students can achieve relaxed attention. Perhaps the easiest and most effective is **diaphragmatic breathing**. In this type of exercise you have the students concentrate on allowing the air to move down into their upper abdomens (as if you are filling your stomach with breath). To practice, put your left hand on your chest and your right hand on your upper abdomen. If you are breathing correctly, your right hand should rise with the inhalation and fall with the exhalation; the left hand should not move. You should feel a slight motion in the lower portion of the chest cavity. The upper portion of your chest should remain still. Do not try to force the breath. Allow the motion to be gentle and effortless. After gaining control of diaphragmatic movement and establishing a smooth, even rhythmic respiration, gently slow down the rate of exhalation until you are breathing out for about twice as long as you are inhaling, e.g., inhale 1 2 3 4 seconds, exhale 1 2 3 4 5 6 7 8 seconds. After you have established this gentle rhythm, stop the mental counting and focus on the smoothness and evenness of the breath flow. In the *Science of Breath*, Swami Rama says, "Rhythmic breathing brings the whole system, including the brain, under perfect harmony and by this means the most perfect condition is obtained for unfoldment of . . . latent faculties."

Here is a guided relaxation breathing exercise you can use if your students are having difficulty.

MIND-SYNCH BREATHING EXERCISE:
— Find a comfortable position . . . relax . . .
— You're letting go of all thoughts . . .
— There is lots of time . . .
— Just clear your mind . . .
— Begin focusing on your breathing . . . P = 15 sec.
— Take a deep breath and slowly exhale . . . P = 10 sec.
— Take another deep breath and allow the air to fill your abdomen . . . P = 10 sec.
— Feel your stomach cavity expand as you inhale . . .
— Feel your stomach cavity move inward as you exhale . . .
— Notice how motionless your chest is . . . as you continue your slow and even breathing . . . P = 15 sec.
— Now concentrate on your diaphragm muscle pushing down as you inhale . . . and floating up on exhalation . . . P = 15 sec.
— I want you now to focus your attention on the air flowing in and out of your nostrils . . . P = 15 sec.
— Feel the coolness on inhalation . . .
— Feel the warmth on exhalation . . .
— Just feel this gentle flow of relaxing air . . . P = 30 sec.
— Your breathing is now smooth and even . . .
— You are calm and comfortable . . . P = 15 sec.

— Alright... you have concluded your breathing exercise... P = 5 sec.
— Begin focusing on your original setting ... P = 5 sec.
— When I count to five you will be back and alert ...
— One-two-three-four-five ...

GUIDED RELAXATION IMAGERY:
Title: Drifting On A Lake
— Find a comfortable position ... relax ... and begin focusing on your breathing ...
— You are lying down in a canoe ...
— Your head is on a soft fluffy pillow ...
— You are calm and comfortable ...
— See yourself in the middle of a beautiful lake ...
— Look at the calmness of the water ...
— See it as still as glass ...
— Feel the sun shining down on you ...
— Feel its warmth on your arms ... legs ... whole body ...
— Listen to the sounds coming from the nearby woods ...
— Hear the birds singing ...
— Listen to the chatter of crickets ...
— Feel a soft cool breeze blowing gently on your face ...
— Feel a very slight swaying as your canoe drifts and drifts ...
— Smell the cleanness in the air ...
— Look up and see a magnificent blue sky with small ruffle-like white clouds moving slowly by ...
— Let your hand float in the cool water ...
— Feel the wet and tingling sensation ...
— Notice how peaceful everything is ...
— Enjoy this comfortable and relaxing place ...
— Look around and see all the beauty of this magnificent place ...
— Alright ... begin to focus on images of your original setting ...
— When I count to five you will be back and alert ...
— One-two-three-four-five ...

GUIDED FANTASY IMAGERY
Title: A Flying Bicycle
— Find a comfortable position ... relax ... and begin focusing on your breathing ...

— See yourself sitting on a shiny new bicycle . . .
— Look at a special switch which allows the bicycle to fly . ..
— Before you fly . . . just ride down the street and get used to your new bike . . .
— Notice how easy it is to pedal . . .
— See the shiny spoked wheels and beautiful colors . . .
— Now it's time to test this magical bike . . .
— Push the special switch . . .
— Feel the bicycle beginning to lift off the ground . . .
— Feel yourself safely lifting up . . . up . . . up into the air . . .
— Feel the excitement . . . as you float over the houses and streets . . .
— Feel the wind blowing against your face . . .
— Look below . . . and see people waving to you . . .
— Notice the amazement on their faces . . .
— Turn and go through a soft white fluffy cloud . . .
— Feel the peace . . . listen to the sounds of silence . . .
— See the beautiful trees and flowers as you peacefully fly above . . .
— It's time to return home . . .
— Turn around and begin coming slowly down . . .
— See your house now below . . .
— You're coming down . . .
— Listen to everyone greeting you . . .
— See the smiles on their faces . . .
— Alright . . . your trip is over . . . begin focusing on images of your original setting . . .
— When I count to five you will be back and alert . . .
— One-two-three-four-five

MEMORY TRAINING SYSTEM 5:
MASTERY SKILL & PERFORMANCE REHEARSAL (MSPR)

DESCRIPTION:
Mastery skill and performance rehearsal is a powerful psychological tool that allows you to take what you would most *like* to do and turn it into what you *will* most likely do. The technique should not be confused with wishful thinking or even positive thinking. Wishful thinking is fantasizing about something you hope is coming true but over which you have little control. Positive thinking is telling yourself you can do it.

Both are concerned with ends rather than the means: you're either hoping for the best or you're attempting to build enough self-confidence to do your best. With MSPH, on the other hand, you are thinking and practicing the doing, the means by which you can give your best possible performance. The more vivid and detailed your images of success are, the better your body can understand what to do. MSPH is an extension of the relaxation and concentration process. It extends concentration in that it carries your focused attention (100% energy) right into the upcoming performance, which might be mastery on a test or mastery of an oral report. It is most important that you always mentally rehearse the correct action or skill, imagine it successfully no matter how much uncertainty or false modesty tempt you. The important thing is for you to rehearse how you perform the Target Skill or Target Performance with absolute perfection, with absolute mastery. You are using this process to overlearn the skill/performance and make it so familiar that under pressure you are most likely to do it automatically because it has become the most familiar and compelling of your responses. Each time you evoke an image of yourself performing a skill successfully you are "imprinting," registering another positive experience in your subconscious mind. When these imprints are deep (the result of high quality imagery) they tend very dramatically to influence your conscious behavior. The student who concentrates on projecting mastery performance images is using the imagination for something remarkable for s/he is not just projecting and imaging, but also preparing the nerves, the muscles, the heart and the mind to unify their physical action toward a single-minded goal.

> "Imagination is by far the most neglected and underdeveloped of the normal abilities of the human mind. It is the forgotten and rusting key to many treasures of the mind."
> Dr. Barbara Brown
> *Supermind*, 1983

HOW CAN MASTERY SKILL AND MASTERY PERFORMANCE IMAGERY BE USED TO ACCELERATE LEARNING AND ACHIEVEMENT?

The major focus of this system is to prepare you emotionally and intellectually for an upcoming academic event (quiz, test, oral report, etc.). Once the Target skill or performance is selected the student then begins to rehearse mentally his or her skill/performance with absolute perfection and mastery. S/he creates images of him or herself actually performing the skill in the exact setting where it will eventually occur. With the help of your imagination, all the actions, all the details will be presented to you in amazing vividness. Every movement will be projected in the most realistic manner.

PREPARATION FOR A TEST:

Preparing for a test is a major responsibility for any student. Success on that test may be determined by the quality of preparation done by the student. How the student feels about the subject matter and about his or her comprehension of the material are crucial for achieving excellence. Here are some steps for using the system of "Mental Rehearsal" to improve test performance:

STEP 1   Be specific in identifying the TARGET SKILL or PERFORMANCE to be imaged, e.g., you should know the exact information that will be required of you on the test.

STEP 2   Create a clear picture of the setting where the test will be taken (furniture, windows, colors, textures, odors, faces, sounds, etc.).

STEP 3   Identify the specific time and date when the test will take place, e.g., Wed., 10:30 AM, Nov. 17.

STEP 4   You are ready to begin your Imagery Rehearsal.

STEP 5   Find a quiet, comfortable setting where you can do your imagery.

STEP 6   Select appropriate background music, e.g., a Baroque or New Age selection. (This is optional, but I recommend the music for its potent, mind-synch, calming effect.)

STEP 7 Decide on the length of time to image.
STEP 8 Use the following imagery exercises:
   A) **Mastery Rehearsal Imagery**
   These images will focus on the process. All of the actions required during test preparation. The activities that one goes through in studying for an upcoming test, e.g., listening, note taking, reading, organizing, questioning, etc. Your imagination knows what's involved, so just let the images float into your awareness.
   Types of Images:
   — Seeing yourself asking your teacher some important questions
   — Observing your excellent listening skills
   — Seeing yourself studying for long periods of time
   — Seeing yourself walking away from a studying session feeling very confident

   B) **Final State Imagery**
   In this exercise the imager focuses on the actual test taking. S/he sees herself or himself performing with perfection, making all the right decisions, answering all the questions correctly, with ease and confidence. The moment has arrived, and the imager is "doing it."
   Types of Images:
   — Seeing yourself in the testing room.
   — Observing yourself responding quickly and accurately.
   — Feeling a high level of confidence.
   — Seeing familiar questions.
   — Listening to yourself making positive comments about how easy the test is.

   C. **Behavioral Consequences Imagery**
   In this exercise the student will focus on images of people reacting positively to the test results. S/he will feel the excitement and the rewards of having done well. S/he will feel the joys of having completed the test, having achieved the goal. The images will center on the situations following this accomplishment.
   Types of Images:
   — Walking out of the test setting and seeing your instructor smile at you.

— Bringing your paper home to your parents and listening to their praise.
— Listening and feeling the congratulations
— Seeing your test score displayed on a bulletin board.

NOTE: Always do each of the above exercises when rehearsing mastery test performance.

ORAL PRESENTATION

Speaking in front of others can create anxiety. The tensions and feelings of uncertainty can lead to inferior performance. An excellent approach in preparing for an oral presentation is Mastery Rehearsal Performance. Imaging perfect performances repeatedly can saturate one's nervous system with a "blue print" for success. Through these repeated mental images a person gains valuable insight into the content, presentation style, modes of response and environmental seating. Each time the image content is repeated the imager receives new information and/or a different perspective. If a student were to image him/herself with perfect performance 100 times, s/he could complements the imagination from a hundred different perspectives. There would be something different, something new, with each image repetition. Come into each image with a clear mind, in a receptive state. Just allow these different perspectives to float into your awareness. A. Ahsen (1977) refers to this phenomenon as the "principle of repetition." This repetition effect can happen with any content being imaged.

Here are three imagery exercises to use in preparing for an oral presentation.

A) Mastery Rehearsal Imagery

In this exercise, concentrate on images of the process of making an excellent oral presentation. All the actions, events, and behaviors relating to the oral presentation will be seen in the form of multiple images.

These visualizations will spontaneously "jump" into the imager's consciousness. The images are usually sequential and highly detailed, presenting an indepth perspective of all that is involved in the real life experience.

Types of Images:
— collecting and organizing all sorts of reference material.

- the actual setting (room, furniture, pictures, colors, sounds, etc.).
- presentation outline.
- feelings of confidence
- specific material to be presented, e.g., a quote, or a list of events, etc.

B) **Final-State Imagery**

The focus of this exercise is on the actual oral presentation being given. The content of these images of mastery deal only with the presentation as it is being given. Maintain concentration on all the variables relating to the actual moment of presentation—the here and now. The imager should create pictures of perfect performance. S/he should see him or herself relaxed, confident, well prepared and handling any unexpected questions or situations that might arise. The imagery should represent the real experience as much as possible.

Types of Images:

- speaking with confidence.
- in command of subject matter.
- the faces of people in the audience.
- material, books, resources, visual-aides, etc.
- positive responses from the audience, especially non-verbal behavior.
- a perfect closing with an audience response.

C) **Behavioral Consequences Imagery**

The aim of this exercise is to create images relating to all the specific reactions from different people involved in the presentation. The reactions of the audience, congratulations received from the teacher, as well as any rewards or specific recognition attained. The focus is on all that occurs following this perfect oral presentation.

Types of Images:
- receiving praise from your mentor.
- a letter or note congratulating you for an excellent presentation.
- a newspaper article.
- someone asking to have the presentation given again.
- talking with your parents and receiving their praise.

If the situation warrants, a student may develop a script and tape for their upcoming event. For example, preparing for the SAT's or making a graduation speech would be significant and would undoubtedly require much study and practice. In these situations one might wish to use this special method of mastery rehearsal imagery via an audio tape recording with a written script.

HOW IS A SCRIPT PREPARED FOR MASTERY PERFORMANCE REHEARSAL?

Preparing a written script is very important as it will serve as the major fuel or nucleus of the imaging content. It will structure and sequence what and when the imager is to image different things relating to the target event. The script should be carefully sequenced and include numerous sensory suggestions in order to bring as much reality to the experience as possible. It should include relaxation suggestions to clear the mind and positive affirmations for making the experience more intense, more emotional and more personal. Here is a sample format for scripting a rehearsal tape:

Tape Section:	Description	Length
A	Relaxing Breathing	1 min.
B	Systematic Body Relaxation	2 mins.
C	Specific content relating to target event (setting, time, people, actions, material, etc.)	5-10 mins.
D	Positive Affirmations	2 mins.
E	Gentle return/count back	30 sec.
	Total	10-15 mins.

If you so desire, the script can be shortened by not including Sections A & B (relaxation) and Section E (positive affirmations). It is important, however, to quiet the mind just prior to beginning rehearsal imagery. High quality imagery is what you want. If your mind hasn't been stilled or if there are lots of distractions, achieving quality imagery may be more difficult.

After the script is written, the next step is to record it onto a cassette tape. You can use your own voice or another person's voice. Be sure you like the voice you hear. Another consideration is whether you would like to have some background music, e.g., Baroque or New Age. The soothing, pleasant, relaxing sounds of this type of music stimulate image production. The length of your rehearsal tape, the content and any background music are all very personal, therefore, choose what you like—whatever works best for you!

WHAT ARE SOME SPECIFIC IMAGERY TECHNIQUES THAT CAN BE USED DURING MASTERY PERFORMANCE REHEARSAL?

There are hundreds of creative manipulations an imager can perform during any rehearsal experience. As you experiment with the process, new ideas will continue to surface. Your bio-computer is infinite. Here are some techniques you can use during your rehearsal exercise:

SLOW MOTION
Description:
> Everything in your programmed imagery is projected in slow motion. Every action, movement is seen in super slow motion.

Benefits:
> It allows the imager to study more carefully each aspect of the target event, resulting in more perceptual insights and more valuable information. Detailed events are illuminated with great clarity.

STOP ACTION
Description:
> At the direction of the imager, a projection can be stopped at any time. Any event or situation can be brought to a "frozen image" sort of like a picture slide.

Benefits:
> It allows the imager time to make some mental observations and perhaps some notes about a specific action of the event. It brings out great detail. Information may be received that might have been overlooked had it not been for the stopped action projection.

IMAGE REPETITION
Description:
> Image content is selected and then viewed in repeated images (10, 15, 20 times). Each repetition will be projected for a designated time period (10 sec., 30 sec., or 1 min.). The images are projected at regular speed in each of the repetitions.

Benefits:
> Each repetition produces new ISM's [I = Image, S = Somatic, M = Meaning] in the form of new information, new ideas, new feel-

ings, new meanings, etc. In addition to gaining valuable insight, there is a positive "imprinting" process going on where the imager's mind is being saturated with visualizations of perfection and mastery. You are conditioning your nervous system.

TRANSFORMATION
Description:
> The imager selects an item, event or situation and then proceeds to change (transform) something within that context, e.g., changing the setting, a person's identity, colors, shapes, sizes, movements, times, . . . anything relating to the target event can be transformed and projected differently.

Benefits:
> It allows the imager to examine cause/effect relationships within the context of their experience. It helps the imager prepare for unexpected changes or circumstances that could occur in the future. You are conditioning the mind to react to these changes in a positive, productive manner.

REVERSE MOTION
Description:
> The imager projects the action in reverse. The content is seen in a sequential manner, only in reverse order. A segment of the content or the entire event can be projected in reverse.

Benefits:
> It allows the imager to analyze the sequential nature of the event, thus being more informed of the unfolding events of a particular experience. The unusual projections may unveil a new and different perspective that might not have surfaced during normal image projection.

SENSORY BOMBARDMENT
Description:
> The imager runs through the entire rehearsal focusing primarily on the sounds, textures, odors, and emotions of his event. The event is seen in its normal occurrence, however, concentration is directed toward all sensory-type experiences.

Benefits:
> It creates and reinforces the reality of the experience. It heightens one's sensitivity to the environment to be encountered. It stimulates the emotions and adds to the intensity of the expectation.

OTHER IMAGE MANIPULATIONS ARE:
> Alternating between Internal and External imagery.
> Using different background music with each image repetition.
> Making major strategy changes in the performance.
> Having a negative event unfolding during the performance.
> Changing the setting.
> Watch someone else do your performance . . . someone with great knowledge and skill . . .
> Seeing different behavioral consequences . . .

> *"A human being always acts and feels and performs in accordance with what he imagines to be true about himself and his environment."*
>
> Dr. Maxwell Maltz
> *Psycho-Cybernetics*, 1963

"Your nervous system cannot tell the difference between an *imagined* experience and a *real* experience. In either case, it reacts automatically to information which you give to it from your forebrain. Your nervous system reacts appropriately to what "you think or imagine to be true" (Maltz, 1963). "Realizing that our actions, feelings and behavior are the result of our own images and beliefs gives us the lever that psychology has always needed for changing personality. It opens a new psychologic door to gaining skill, success and happiness." Scientists tell us that the engrams within our brains can be changed or modified—like a tape recording may be changed by "dubbing in" additional material or like replacing an old recording with a new recording over it. These engrams in the human brain tend to change slightly each time they are "played back." Isn't that fantastic! Each time you do a positive rehearsal you are enriching those engrams of your brain that govern the specific actions of your performance.

The engrams take on some of the tone and temper of our present mood, thinking and attitudes toward them. That's why we play positives over and over—we are saturating our brain so that it can only function in one way . . . the *winning* way!

Our present thinking, our present mental habits, our attitudes toward past experiences, and our attitudes toward the future—all have a profound influence upon old recorded engrams.

Replace those old recordings with new ones. Make your new tapes, powerful, exciting, "best sellers." Your mind thirsts for a winning tape. And when your new tape is ready, play the heck out of it. You'll be amazed at how your behavior will follow the script. For best results you should practice your imagery exercises on a daily basis or at least five times per week. If you are looking for more dramatic and immediate changes, then you must do your imagery a few times a day. Once you become familiar with the imagery process you will be able to determine how much effort is needed to produce the desired outcome.

MASTERY PERFORMANCE REHEARSAL ACTIVITIES

Describe your Mastery Rehearsal Performance: (Target Event)

_____

_____

_____

_____

_____

_____

_____

The following is a list of specific imagery exercises to be used in performance rehearsal:

Mastery Performance Rehearsal Imagery
Repetition
Final-State Imagery
Behavioral Consequences Imagery
Slow Motion
Reverse Motion
Transformation
Sensory Bombardment
Internal Imagery

External Imagery

Stop Action
Other Person
Imaging Music

Note: Write in the correct title for each exercise that you do. The ISM response is any reaction, description of image, description of feelings, new meanings, ideas, questions, etc., that you receive during the image exercise. Include the length of time for the image exercise.

Imagery Exercise # 1

Title: _____ Time _____

ISM Response _____

_____

_____

_____

_____

_____

Imagery Exercise # 2

Title: _____ Time _____

ISM Response _____

_____

_____

_____

_____

_____

Imagery Exercise # 3

Title: _____ Time _____

ISM Response _____

_____

_____

_____

_____

_____

_____

Imagery Exercise # 4

Title: _____ Time _____

ISM Response _____

_____

_____

_____

_____

_____

_____

Mastery Performance Rehearsal Follow-Up

List of ideas generated through Mastery Performance Rehearsal:

1. _____

2. _____

3. _____

4. _____

5. _____

Answer the following:

1. How long do I want each rehearsal experience to be? _____

2. Do I want it to be guided _____ non-guided _____ or both _____ ?

3. Do I want to use my voice _____ or another person's voice _____ for my guided rehearsal?

4. When will I do my guided rehearsal? _____

5. How long should my rehearsal be? _____

6. What creative techniques do I want to use in my exercises?

   _____

7. What type of music do I want to hear during my exercises?

   _____

   _____

Action Steps (actions taken after imagery experience):

1. _____
2. _____
3. _____
4. _____
5. _____

Mastery Performance Rehearsal Script For Target Event:

_____
_____
_____
_____
_____
_____
_____
_____
_____
_____
_____

Type of Relaxation: _____

Length of Tape: _____

Type of Background Music _____

List of Positive Affirmations: _____

_____

_____

_____

_____

_____

_____

"There is a powerful and mysterious force in human nature that is capable of bringing about dramatic improvement in our lives. It is a kind of mental engineering that works best when supported by strong faith. It's not difficult to practice; anyone can do it. Recently it has caught the attention of doctors, psychologists, and thinkers everywhere, and a new word has been coined to describe it. That is imaging, derived from imagination. An image formed and held tenaciously in the conscious mind will pass presently, by a process of mental osmosis, into the unconscious mind. And when it is accepted firmly in the unconscious, the individual will strongly tend to have it, for then it has you. So powerful is the imaging effect on thought and performance that a long-held visualization of an object or goal can become determinative. Imaging is positive thinking carried one step further."

Dr. Norman Vincent Peale
Positive Imaging, 1983

MEMORY TRAINING SYSTEM 6:
MENTAL SCREEN

DESCRIPTION:
Everything you wish to remember is associated with some previous event. If it is a name, the event is the time you heard or read it. All you have to do, once you learn to work with your mental screen, is to visualize a past event that surrounds an incident you believe you have forgotten, and it will be there. The key is not to try to press the mind into remembering the specific fact, but to allow it to emerge while concentrating on the event associated with or related to the fact. Again with reference to remembering a name, you would create your mental screen and begin projecting images of the event where the name appeared or happened. The images are evoked in a relaxed state of mind. Whatever sequence the imagination dictates is the way one will observe the images. While viewing these images in a passive frame of mind the name or object needing to be remembered may just pop into your head . . . and all of a sudden you have it! Most of us try too hard to remember something. We try to force the issue, going right at it. The "mental screen" of this system takes us there—but through a different route.

STEPS FOR USING MENTAL SCREEN
1. Develop a setting where you can activate your personal viewing screen, e.g., creative workshop, Bagley (1987). It can be any environment that you like, indoors or out-of-doors, in any location as long as you use the same setting for mental screen imagery.
2. Determine which event you are going to project onto your mental screen. This will be the event associated with what you are in need of remembering. It can be all the activities of a particular day, a special place, or a certain conversation you had with another person.
3. Do a brief relaxation just to clear your mind.
4. In a comfortable position, relaxed, allow your event to unfold in whatever manner your imagination chooses. Just be patient. Don't look for the answer right away. Allow the associative processes of the mind time to blend and interact. Although you have an expectation that you will remember what you need to . . . you must stay in an unhurried relaxed attitude.

5. The illumination arrives—your data are remembered. The information you have been expecting floats into your awareness.
6. Before leaving the exercise, take one more look at your setting and in particular your mental screen. This is important as you want to develop a very familiar and positive feeling about your personalized setting.
7. Leave your mental screen and slowly return to your original setting.

The mental screen method is effective when you need to remember a specific detail of the past. Remember, become familiar with your mental screen, its features, its location and how it operates. The more you use it the more effective it becomes.

MEMORY TRAINING SYSTEM 7:
PERSONAL INFORMATION PROCESSING SYSTEM (PIPS)

DESCRIPTION:
Each of us has a unique and different system for processing information from our environment. Our perceptual abilities differ in that we see and analyze things according to a highly personal and individual set of learning experiences. We think differently, we learn differently and we react differently to the situations and circumstances that we meet daily.

In this system we will explore these thinking and learning differences through a creative process that involves
a) how information is brought into our minds
b) how this information is categorized and filed in our minds and
c) how this stored information is then retrieved from our minds.

The objective of this exploration is to have you creatively develop your PERSONAL INFORMATION PROCESSING SYSTEM (PIPS). Once your PIPS is developed you can use it for memorizing data. It then becomes another means for processing information.

There are three separate activities in creating your PIPS. We will use a guided imagery exercise in each of the three activities. The activities should be done during one session or classroom period. Let's begin with phase one of PIPS.

PHASE ONE:
HOW INFORMATION IS BROUGHT INTO OUR MINDS

INSTRUCTIONS:
In this phase you are to create a highly imaginative means for the manner in which information is brought into your mind. During the guided image you will be encouraged to see and experience this processing of information in the most creative way.

The idea is to have you not only develop a personal system for processing information but to make this system very creative and unique. So let your imagination fly, be creative, be spontaneous.

PHASE ONE:
GUIDED IMAGERY EXERCISE

— Find a comfortable position ... relax ... and begin focusing on your breathing ...
— Clear your mind ...
— You are letting go of all thoughts ...
— There is lots of time ...
— I want you just to allow yourself to be as creative as you have ever been ...
— Your imagination is willing and ready to be creative ...
— Alright ... it is now time to focus on creative images ...
— I want you now to see in the most creative manner ... just how you bring information into you mind ... P = 30 sec.
— Alright ... just relax for a moment ... P = 15 sec.
— Again ... see your creative process for bringing in information ... P = 30 sec.
— You now have this personal creative process ... complete ...
— It is yours ... there is nothing else like it ...
— You can go to it at any time ... make any changes you like ...
— Let us now return to your original setting ...
— When I count to five ... you will be back and alert ...
— One-two-three-four-five ...

PHASE ONE:
GUIDED IMAGERY EXERCISE-CREATIVE RESPONSE DESCRIPTION
(How your mind brings in information)
ISM Response

_____

_____

_____

_____

_____

_____

_____

_____

_____

_____

PHASE TWO:
HOW INFORMATION IS CATEGORIZED AND FILED IN YOUR MIND

Instructions:
In Phase Two you are to go through a similar process, only this time the focus will be on developing a **creative** means for categorizing and filing information, once it has been received in the mind. It can be a continuation of the creative system developed in phase one or it can be an entirely new system. It can be related or it can be different. Again, the key is to be creative with whatever system you develop. The guided imagery exercise will be similar to the Phase One exercise.

PHASE TWO:
GUIDED IMAGERY EXERCISE

— Find a comfortable position ... relax ... and begin focusing on your breathing ...
— Let all of your thoughts ... go ...
— Clear your mind ...
— There is lots of time ...
— In a moment you are going to allow your creativity to emerge ...
— Alright ... I want you now to develop a creative process for how your mind categorizes and files information ... P = 30
— Now relax for a moment ... P = 15 sec.
— Again ... I want you to see very clearly the creative means in which your mind categorizes and files information ...
— Your creative process is now established ...
— You may go back to it at any time and make any changes you like ...
— Begin to focus on images of your original setting ...
— When I count to five you will be back and alert ...
— One-two-three-four-five

PHASE TWO:
GUIDED IMAGERY EXERCISE
CREATIVE RESPONSE DESCRIPTION
(Categorizing and Filing Information)

ISM Response: _____

_____

_____

_____

_____

PHASE THREE:
HOW INFORMATION IS RETRIEVED FROM YOUR MIND

INSTRUCTIONS:
In this final phase you are to develop a creative process for the way your mind retrieves information from your filing system. Again, the system can be different from the other phases or it can be related. You are to allow your imagination to develop a creative means for retrieving information. Be spontaneous, be creative. Allow yourself to relax and follow the guided imagery exercise.

PHASE THREE:
GUIDED IMAGERY EXERCISE

— Find a comfortable position . . . relax . . . and begin focusing on your breathing . . .
— You are letting go of all thoughts . . .
— There is lots of time . . .
— Just focus on your breathing . . .
— In a moment you are going to allow your creativity to emerge . . .
— Alright . . . I want you now to develop a creative means for how your mind retrieves filed information . . . P = 30 sec.
— Just relax now for a moment . . . P = 15 sec.
— Again . . . see your creative retrieval system . . . clearly and vividly . . . P = 15 sec.
— Notice the creative way your mind retrieves information . . .
— You now have your creative retrieval system . . . you may go to it at any time and make any changes you like . . .
— Begin focusing on images of your original setting
— When I count to five you will be back and alert . . .
— One-two-three-four-five

PHASE THREE:
GUIDED IMAGERY EXERCISE
CREATIVE RESPONSE DESCRIPTION
(How Information is Retrieved From the Mind)

ISM Response: _____

_____

_____

_____

_____

You now have successfully completed the three phases of your PIPS system. Here are some activities to use with PIPS:

1. Illustrate your PIPS through a creative drawing.
2. Describe the complete system in detail.
3. Use your PIPS with a single data unit first, then try it with several data units.
4. Return to your PIPS via imagery and make any changes you like.
5. Describe the creative process you used in the development of PIPS.
6. Make a list of all the different ways PIPS can be used.
7. Have students compare and contrast their different PIPS systems.

MEMORY TRAINING SYSTEM 8:
KEYWORD METHOD

DESCRIPTION:

The most widely employed and researched mnemonic device is the "Keyword Method." The approach was first utilized to accelerate the learning of a foreign language. The process involves generating an interactive image of the word to be learned and an English "sound alike." For instance, the Spanish word for "record" is "disco." To remember this the learner would visualize "Disco Dan" playing a record at a music hop. The first part of this dual-coding system is the associative word "Dan." The second part is the action image of "Disco Dan" playing a record. Atkinson (1975) is credited with the formualtion of this system, however, Pressley (1977, 1982, 1983, 1984) has been recognized as the person most actively involved with its application to learning and memory and research.

The keyword method is a variant of Paivio's (1971) "Pegword" method, Sheinen (1985). In the Peg-word method the student pre-learns rhymed pairs such as "one-bun, two-shoe, four-soar," etc. To recall objects in ordinal position they would then be associated with a pre-learned "peg." Sheinen (1985) provides an example "if five-hive is the mnemonic key, then the fifth word on the list, perhaps car, would be associated with hive." One could visualize a car driving into a huge bee hive, or a car adorned with bee hives.

Both the "Peg-word" and the "Key-word" methods apply a dual-coding process. The first process involves the association of a target word with another word. The concept is that the key-word will assist the learner in remembering the target word. The associated word is a sound-a-like or rhyming-type word. Both serve as effective cues for triggering recall. If the associated word is a personalized type of word or some crazy, ridiculous word it will increase memorization. This occurs on the basis of motivation and original awareness for the association. The second part of the dual-coding process is the creation of an action mental image involving the associated word.

Here is an example:

Target Word Image	Word Association	Action
disco (record)	Dan	Disco Dan playing a record at the music hop
five	hive	A car driving into a huge bee hive

Most researchers agree that action-type images of high vividness are remembered better than non-action images of lower quality and vividness. The combination of word association and image association has been found to enhance learning and memory Sheinen (1985). Pressley, Levin and Delaney (1982) reviewed the key-word method exclusively and found it to be effective in increasing memory of definitions, enhancing comprehension, and improving factual recall in science and social studies. Many of the memory training exercises found in Chapter 3 incorporate the principles of the dual-coding theory.

Key-word Method Exercise:

Make a list of ten target words. For each word develop a word association (a sound-a-like, rhyming word, etc.). Finally, create an action-type image for each of the words.

Target Word Image   **Word Association**   **Action**

1.

2.

3.

4.

5.

6.

7.

8.

9.

10.

MEMORY TRAINING SYSTEM 9:
LINK SYSTEM

DESCRIPTION:
The system involves linking one item to be remembered to another item, forming the links of a memory chain. One item must lead you to the next, if you're associating properly. The Link system, according to H. Lorayne (1974), is used to remember things in sequence. A speech is a sequence of thoughts, a formula is a sequence of components, any number with more than two digits is a sequence. There are two steps involved. First you need a ridiculous—impossible, crazy, illogical, absurd—picture or image to associate the two items that are to be remembered. What you don't want is a logical or sensible picture. Lorayne provides an example in his book, *The Memory Book*. A ridiculous or impossible picture might be a gigantic tree flying instead of an airplane, or an airplane growing instead of the tree, or airplanes growing on trees. The second step is to select one of the pre-determined pictures and begin evoking mental images in the mind's eye.

The Four Rules Of Linking:

A) Substitution—picture one item instead of the other (see the tree flying instead of the airplane).
B) Out of Proportion—try to see the items larger than life. (Use the words gigantic, monstrous, etc.)
C) Exaggeration—whenever the word "millions" is used you are forced to apply your imagination.
D) Action—action is always easy to remember.

Making the pictures ridiculous is what enables you to really see them; a logical picture is usually too vague. Once you really see the ridiculous picture, it does register in your mind.

LINKING SYSTEM EXERCISE:
Make a list of words which are sequential and place them in the ITEM columns below (thoughts from a speech, a formula, a series of digits). Then create a ridiculous picture for each set of items and allow images to come into your mind.

Describe:

COLUMN A ITEMS	COLUMN B ITEMS	PICTURE LINK
1.	1.	1.
2.	2.	2.
3.	3.	3.
4.	4.	4.
5.	5.	5.
6.	6.	6.
7.	7.	7.
8.	8.	8.
9.	9.	9.
10.	10.	10.

Describe each of your ridiculous picture link images. Remember take item one word and link it with item two word in a ridiculous manner. Through the Link System you will learn how to make any intangible thing, any abstract piece of information, tangible and meaningful in your mind.

MEMORY TRAINING SYSTEM 10:
PERSONAL TRIGGERING SYSTEM (PTS)

DESCRIPTION:
This system involves a simple triggering mechanism which, once it becomes really yours, improves effectiveness as you use it. Making it yours will require several relaxation-imagery sessions to internalize thoroughly the procedure. Here are four triggering mechanism categories:

First: Visual Cue
   This can be any visual stimulus that a person can see at all times. For the Visual Cue to be effective it must be in a person's view or in the proximity of that person. It must be reachable or obtainable when needed.
Examples
   a ring, watch symbol, a graphic design, a painting, a marking, a button, any man-made object, an abstract picture, etc.

Second: Word
   This can be any word that a person selects as his or her triggering device. The word should be personal, perhaps unusual. It can be a fictitious word. Whatever appeals to you. You must like it.
Examples
   Orange, forest, bird, dynamic, fruitful, sing-song, hydro, turnout, yregami (imagery backwards), etc.

Third: Image
   Here a person develops a short special visualization of something pleasurable. The image can be of anything or anybody. It may be seen anywhere, at any time. It should be a personal image that one enjoys and can relate to the triggering mechanism.

Examples
   An image of nature, something powerful, something spiritual, funny, high tech., something with great speed, etc.

Fourth: Action
> This is something a person can perform. It can be any special movement that a person makes. It is a designated action specifically used for triggering one's recall system.

Examples
> Having your two fingers touch, an arm position, a body position, tapping the arm gently and repeatedly, slow head turn or movement, etc.

The important point here is that the personalized triggering mechanism must be originated by you. It must be something that you really enjoy. If you select a PTS and then want to change it, that's O.K.

Here are some suggestions for making your triggering device an effective Memory Training System:

1. Find a device or cue that really motivates you, something original.

2. Put yourself into a relax state of mind, evoke images of your triggering device in action and images of you being successful.

3. Use your triggering device daily. Make it part of your daily routine.

4. Practice using it when you need to recall something.

5. Develop a strong belief in the system—a belief that it will work.

6. Develop an expectation that your triggering system will improve your recall and memory.

7. Practice . . . practice . . . practice . . .

8. Keep it private. Don't share with other people.

9. When you feel that the system is helping you, write about it. Keep a journal.

REMEMBER: This is something you can have the rest of your life.

For What Situations Can I Use My Personal Triggering System?

1. Trying to recall someone's name.

2. Remembering a fact or answer to a test question.

3. When I want to remember something important.

4. As a prerequisite to any learning situation.

5. I can think about its effectiveness when I daydream.

6. While reading important information or certain sections of the text.

7. During a lesson as the teacher is giving out important facts.

Note: Your PTS must be practiced during mind relaxation in order to internalize thoroughly the procedure.

CHAPTER 3
INTRODUCTION TO MEMORY – IMAGERY EXERCISES

In this Chapter there are twenty-one Memory exercises using mental imagery. The exercises are presented in random order. Selection should be based on teacher-student interest. Success in the Memory exercises will largely depend on how imagery was introduced to the class and the environment for conducting the experiences. If time was taken to discuss the image process thoroughly (in the form of group discussion and feedback sessions) and students were given several introductory image experiences, the exercises will be highly successful in demonstrating how to increase one's memory skills. Prior to beginning the memory exercises students should be given time to become familiar with the Memory Terms and Concepts presented in the next section.

Memory-Imagery Exercises - Terms and Concepts

IMAGER—A person engaged in the creative act of evoking mental images in the form of pictures, feelings and meanings. The student is projecting images on his/her viewing screen of the mind.

IMAGE PROJECTION—The process of projecting (evoking) an image onto one's viewing screen which is the mind's eye. The projection concept is used to reinforce the idea that the imager is like a projectionist capable of speeding up, slowing down, stilling, reversing, etc., an image. It is the picture one sees as one concentrates on the mind's screen.

IMAGE SET—A verbal cue signifying that the guided image exercise is to begin. It alerts the imager that the next set of suggestions are about to be presented.

PROJECTION SCREEN—A large screen used by the student for projecting his/her images. The screen can be of any design and have any features the imager would like. The same screen should always be used so that familiarity is established, making it easier to return.

FADE-IN—The process of having an image slowly come into focus. It is the gradual, unfolding of the image onto the screen of the mind's eye.

FADE-OUT—The process of having an image slowly dissolve or disappear from one's viewing screen.

PAUSE (P)—In each of the memory exercises you will find the symbol (P) indicating that there is a recommended pause at that moment. The teacher or instructor remains silent for the length of time indicated after the P, e.g., P = 15 seconds. No verbal suggestions will be made for fifteen seconds.

TARGET DATA (TD)—This is the specific information to be memorized. It is all the material or information that will be presented during the exercise. It may be a list of names, a vocabulary list, numbers, or any other material. The target data should be carefully selected and should not exceed an appropriate amount for the particular exercise.

DATA UNIT—This is the unit of data to be processed during a single image projection. It is one single piece of information. It may be a name, date, word, place, object, event, thing, etc.

PREARRANGED DATA—This represents the data to be used in the memory exercise. It is the exact order in which the data will appear.

What Is Imagery?

The image has been identified in psychological literature as a vision, as a source for new thought and feeling, as a material picture in the mind which can be scanned by the person as s/he would scan a real current event in his/her environment, and as a potent highly significant stimulus which arises from within the mind and throws it into a series of self-revealing effects Richardson (1968) and Ahsen (1977). It is a method which uses spontaneous and multi-potential images (pictures) instead of words for exposure to new life-related emotions and ideas.

Major Image Components—ISM Model

The image consists of three major components: The (I) image which is the picture, visualization; the (S) somatic response, which is the emotional or feeling message received from the images; and the (M) meaning, which is the conceptual idea, perception or new thought generated, Ahsen (1977). Imagery is a highly "creative act" most effective for gaining new ideas, reinforcing learned concepts, and retrieving information stored in our mental libraries. The ISM construct is what makes imagery such a powerful tool for thinking, learning, and living.

Types of Images

There are basically three classifications of images: Dream, Memory and Imagination. The last two are the functional ones we use for imagery learning. Dream images are considered to be our most potent and vivid pictures. For instructional imagery purposes, dream imagery is less effective for using in thinking and learning activities. The most popular type is the Memory image. Here a person can actively call upon a previous experience in attempting to remember certain facts or details. Memory images are usually evoked by a sensory stimulus, a verbal utterance, a picture, or a certain taste, or smell. The third imagery type is Imagination Imagery. It is different from memory images in that it has no fixed reference point. Imagination images are spontaneous, free, unstructured, creative experiences integrating past experiences with present experiences in newly organized patterns. The imagination image will be the vehicle we will use in the memory exercises to follow. It is this image type (imagination) that is motivating, exciting, different—all the important ingredients for "imprinting" data into our minds.

How Are the Memory-Imagery Exercises Used?

Each of the twenty-one exercises are divided into five parts. They consist of:
a) Memory Technique Description,
b) Guided Imagery Exercise Instructions,
c) Non-guided Imagery Exercise Instructions,
d) Variations, and
e) Follow-up Activities.

PART 1 **Memory Technique Description**
This provides the instructor with a general description of the focus for the exercise, including suggestions for preparing students through relaxation activities, discussion periods, etc. These instructions can be altered to meet the needs of the teacher or interests of the students. They are important and must be explained to the students prior to beginning the exercise.

PART 2 **Guided Imagery Exercise Instructions**
This is the sequence of verbal suggestions that will be spoken to the students once they are relaxed and focused. The suggestions will help the students evoke, control and manipulate their data images in strange, unusual, and creative ways—thus increasing the probability of information retention. The exercises are from 5 to 15 minutes. Background music is recommended for several of the exercises. Instructors should read thoroughly the guided suggestions and in some cases practice before administering to the class. Use different voice inflections where appropriate, and be sure to pause for an appropriate time, especially where long pauses are recommended, e.g., 15 sec., 30 sec. The more experience you have with guided imagery, the better you become at determining when, where, and how long to pause.

PART 3 **Non-guided Imagery Exercise Instructions**
This is an alternative exercise to the guided imagery. Same technique, only no spoken suggestions are given. The students simply follow the technique procedures and de-

cide on what data to project and how long the projection image should last. Non-guided imagery is essential for learning and memory, therefore, you should encourage students to experience this type of imagery frequently. Allow students the flexibility to control and direct their imagery.

PART 4   **Variations**
For each memory exercise there are at least four specific variations that you can use with the activities. Always read the variations first, to determine if there are some changes or modifications you would like to make. Also, be sure to write and use any additional variations that come to mind.

PART 5   **Follow-up Activities**
Each memory exercise should have a follow-up activity even if it is only a few minutes to write some image responses. Feel free to modify any of the suggestions. A good idea would be to have students keep a Memory Journal, which could be updated periodically.

SUGGESTIONS FOR USING THE MEMORY-IMAGERY EXERCISES

1. Teach your students how to relax their minds and bodies prior to doing the memory exercises.

2. Fully explain the nature of the memorization process—give examples and allow for discussion.

3. Be thoroughly familiar with the exercise prior to administering it to your students.

4. Rehearse the guided image—practice using different voice inflections and most importantly, learn how to "shut up" during pauses.

5. Provide the students with some short introductory imagery exercises (both guided and non-guided) prior to the memory exercises. [See *200 Ways Of Using Imagery In The Classroom* (Bagley & Hess,

1982) and *Using Imagery In Creative Problem Solving* (Bagley, 1987)]

6. Have the students keep a Memory Journal for recording memory image responses.

7. Always provide opportunities for students to share and discuss their image experiences—however, don't call on them as imagery is, like "art," very personal—it's better for one to offer a comment.

8. Tell your students not to overanalyze or evaluate their images. Allow the images to come and go. Absorb what you like and let go of uninteresting images.

MEMORY EXERCISE:
GRAPHIC VISUAL

MEMORY TECHNIQUE DESCRIPTION:
After selecting the target data, students will be guided through a process in which they will create a different graphic visual (an imaginary image) for each unit of data. When the signal is given the student will create this image whereby s/he will visualize a graphic illustration for the data being memorized. The graphic visual can be any size, shape, texture, style or color and can be creatively seen anywhere the imager chooses.

The imager may use the same graphic visual for each data unit or may select a different graphic visual for each data unit being memorized. The imager must clearly see the word, thing, object, etc., within the structure of the graphic illustration.

GUIDED IMAGERY EXERCISE INSTRUCTIONS:
— Find a comfortable position ... relax ... and begin focusing on your breathing.
— Let all of your thoughts go ... Clear your mind ...
— Activate your concentration energy system P = 15 sec.
— You are now ready to begin ...
— Remember for each data unit you are to create a special graphic visual.
— You will see your data clearly within the structure of your creative graphic.
— Alright ... now let us begin with your data.
— Each time you hear the command "image" you will create the graphic and see it for FIVE seconds and then relax for SEVEN seconds.
— Ready ...
— Image ... P = 7 sec.
— Image ... P = 7 sec.
— Image ... P = 7 sec.
— Image ... P = 7 sec.
— Image ... P = 7 sec.
— Image ... P = 7 sec.
[NOTE: Continue this command for as many repetitions as you like.]
— Alright ... you have completed your images.
— You have created graphic visuals for your data.
— Your data are now permanently filed in your memory system.

— Begin focusing on images of your original setting.
— When I count to five you will be back and alert.
— One-two-three-four-five.

NON-GUIDED IMAGERY EXERCISE INSTRUCTIONS:
Students are to select target data. Give them a time period for completing the exercise. Instruct the class to pause between data units. Encourage the students not to do more than ten data units. Ask the students to decide whether they will use the same styled graphic visual for each data unit or different graphic visuals for each of the images. Tell the students to be creative with their images spending at least ten seconds with each image projection.

VARIATIONS:
A) Provide the students with specific features to incorporate into each of the graphic visual image projections, e.g., color, texture, location, sound, material, etc.
B) Have the students use a completely different graphic system for each data unit.
C) Select one data unit and do repeated graphic visual images, e.g., ten repetitions at fifteen second intervals.
D) Have the students take a graphic visual that has been created and produce it in several different locations.

FOLLOW-UP ACTIVITIES:
A) Describe in detail each graphic visual created.
B) Draw, illustrate, or paint a picture of a particular graphic visual.
C) Write a story about "My Most Exciting Image."
D) Create a musical theme to compliment a particular graphic visual.

MEMORY EXERCISE:
IMPRINTING

MEMORY TECHNIQUE DESCRIPTION:
In this exercise the imager will select a means or specific process for imprinting his/her data into a designated surface. When the student has decided on the imprinting process s/he selects a particular surface, e.g., wood, metal, concrete, where the imprinting action will take place. Each of the pre-selected target data (TD) will be imprinted according to the process and surface determined by the imager. Instruct the students to use the same imprinting process throughout the exercise. The imprinting process and/or surfaces for imprinting can be changed or modified in future memory exercises.

GUIDED IMAGERY EXERCISE INSTRUCTIONS:
— Find a comfortable position ... relax ... and begin focusing on your breathing ...
— Let all of your thoughts ... go ...
— Clear your mind ...
— Activate your concentration energy system ...
— You are now ready to begin.
— Let your attention focus on your special imprinting process.
— Just observe its dynamic action.
— Notice its potent imprinting power.
— Now focus on your designated surface.
— See its color ... detail ... shape.
— Now take a practice word and imprint it into your designated surface.
— Just observe your imprinting power
— Alright ... now let us begin with your data.
— Each time you hear the command you will imprint for five seconds and then relax for seven seconds.
— READY ...
— IMPRINT ... P = 7 sec.
— IMPRINT ... P = 7 sec.
— IMPRINT ... P = 7 sec.
— IMPRINT ... P = 7 sec.
— IMPRINT ... P = 7 sec.
— IMPRINT ... P = 7 sec.

[NOTE: Continue this command for as many repetitions as you like.]
— Alright ... you have completed imprinting your data.
— Your data are now permanently filed in your memory system.
— Begin focusing on images of your original setting.
— When I count to five you will be back and alert.
— One-two-three-four-five.

NON-GUIDED IMAGERY EXERCISE INSTRUCTIONS:
Discuss imprinting process with students. Have each student select an imprint technique and a designated surface. Give example: for imprinting, hot iron; for surface, a piece of white pine. Next, have the students make a list of the data to be memorized. Give them a designated time period for doing their imprinting (3-5 mins.). Instruct the students to be quiet until the exercise has been completed.

VARIATIONS:
A) Have students use a teacher-selected imprinting technique and a designated surface.
B) Have class experiment with different imprinting techniques.
C) With the guided imagery use sensory statements in between imprint commands, e.g., feel the imprint, listen to the sounds of the imprint, etc.
D) Vary the length of time for imprints and pauses during one exercise and with different imprinting exercises.

FOLLOW-UP ACTIVITIES:
A) Make a data list and a corresponding imprinting image response list.
B) Describe your imprinting process.
C) Draw-illustrate the dynamic action of your imprinting technique.
D) Have students discuss the process in small groups.
E) Make-up a special imprinting booklet.

MEMORY EXERCISE:
PICTURE ASSOCIATION

MEMORY TECHNIQUE DESCRIPTION:
In this exercise the imager will use his/her pre-selected target data and allow picture associations to develop in the form of images. The imager will first focus on the data unit for approximately five seconds. Then the imager will take a deep breath followed by a picture image association with the data unit. The picture should just float effortlessly into the imager's awareness. Allow the imager approximately ten seconds to focus on the associated picture. This will be followed by a command to "clear your mind and relax." After a brief pause the next data unit will be projected.

The same process will be followed for each data unit. The key is to not force the picture images, but to just allow them to develop in a relaxed, receptive manner.

GUIDED IMAGERY EXERCISE INSTRUCTIONS:
— Find a comfortable position ... relax ... and begin focusing on your breathing ...
— Let all of your thoughts ... go ...
— Clear your mind...
— Activate your concentration energy system.
— You are now ready to begin.
— Begin to focus on your first data unit P = 5 sec.
— Alright let go of the data unit and take a deep breath P = 5 sec.
— Now allow your picture association image to come into focus P = 10 sec.
— Clear your mind and relax ... P = 10 sec.
— Alright next data unit ... P = 5 sec.
— Let go and take a deep breath P = 5 sec.
— Image ... P = 10 sec. (picture assoc. image).
— Clear your mind and relax P = 10 sec.
[NOTE: Follow the four steps for each data unit in the exercise (do not exceed twenty data units). Four steps:
1. Image the data unit
2. Take a deep breath

3. Image picture association
4. Clear mind and relax]
— Alright you have finished this exercise.
— Your data are now permanently filed in your memory system.
— Begin to focus on images of your original setting.
— When I count to five you will be back and alert.
— One-two-three-four-five.

NON-GUIDED IMAGERY EXERCISE INSTRUCTIONS:
Have students select target data. Tell them the approximate length of time for each picture association image as well as the time allotted for the exercise. Remind them to allow the picture image being associated with the data to float freely into their minds. Don't force the image. Encourage them to be spontaneous and to create different types and styles of images for each data unit. Any picture image evoked while relating data is OK. There is no right or wrong image. It is a personal association being created.

VARIATIONS:
A) Use different lengths of time for any or all of the steps in the exercise.
B) After each picture association have students record (write or draw) their image responses, then go back to next data units followed by another response period (give them 3 or 4 mins. per response.)
C) Use a designated category for picture associations, e.g., images of nature, technological images, etc.
D) Use one picture association theme for all the data to be memorized in the exercise.

FOLLOW-UP ACTIVITIES:
A) Make a list of the target data and corresponding picture associations.
B) Select one picture association image and describe it in detail.
C) Describe how each picture association image unfolded.
D) Discuss "My Strangest Picture Association."
E) Select an art medium and reproduce one of your picture association images.

MEMORY EXERCISE:
MENTAL WALK

MEMORY TECHNIQUE DESCRIPTION:
This exercise requires each student to select a particular familiar route which can be used in the mental walk. Students should select a route that will take them from their house and travel five to ten blocks away. The exercise will involve creating an image of the corner of each block where the imager will visualize his or her data. At the end of each block, at the corner, the imager will see his or her data unit creatively displayed. This process will be repeated at each of the corners (number of blocks should be pre-determined). Students should be encouraged to create a different visual display for each data unit being visualized at the specific location or corner of block.

GUIDED IMAGERY EXERCISE INSTRUCTIONS:
— Find a comfortable position . . . relax . . . and begin focusing on your breathing . . .
— Let all of your thoughts . . . go . . . Clear your mind.
— Activate your concentration energy system.
— You are now ready to begin.
— You have selected your target data.
— Begin now by seeing yourself walking from your house . . .
— You are beginning a special walk.
— At the end of each block you are going to display creatively one data unit.
— Start your walk . . . P = 10 sec.
— You now have reached the end of the first block.
— Creatively display your first data unit
— See it clearly . . . P = 15 sec.
— Now continue your walk
— You now have reached the end of block two.
— Again creatively display a new data unit . . . P = 15 sec.
— Now continue your walk
[NOTE: Give the imager 15 sec. between blocks and 15 sec. for image projection. These pauses can be modified if you like, e.g., 10 sec. or 20 sec.]

— Block # 3
— Block # 4
— Block # 5
— Block # 6
— Block # 7
— Block # 8
— Block # 9
— Block # 10
— You have now reached the end of your walk ... slowly return home going back through each of your blocks.
— See each data unit displayed at each corner block.
— Begin ...Block # 10 ... P = 5 sec.
[Continue back through blocks 9—1 pausing 5 sec. between blocks.]
— You have arrived home.
— You have successfully placed important data at designated points along your route.
— Your data are now permanently filed in your memory system.
— Begin focusing on images of your original setting.
— When I count to five you will be back and alert.
— One-two-three-four-five.

NON-GUIDED IMAGERY EXERCISE INSTRUCTIONS:
Have the students select target data and designated area where there are blocks in which they can take their mental walk. Provide instructions on the procedures for creatively displaying the data at each corner of their walk. Instructions should include
a) time for placing each data unit
b) time between each block and
c) time allotted for the exercise.
Remind the students that they can create whatever image they like at each of the corners. Be creative, be different.

VARIATIONS:
A) Instead of blocks use familiar points in one's neighborhood, e.g., a local street, a friend's house, a section of a park.
B) Select different geographical locations throughout the world.
C) Once the data unit is placed at the designated area have the students use other image processes to reinforce memorization, e.g., repeated images, multi-sensory, etc.
D) Leave more than a single data unit at each location.

E) Repeat the same mental walk several times using the same data and the same imagery.

FOLLOW-UP ACTIVITIES:
A) Describe your particular walk in detail.
B) List and describe each creative display image.
C) Make a list of other geographical locations where one might do a mental walk.
D) Make a list of all the different ways creatively to display data.
E) Write about "My Strangest Image," "My Most Colorful Image," etc.

MEMORY EXERCISE:
LASER FOCUS

MEMORY TECHNIQUE DESCRIPTION:
In this exercise the student will create a special "beam of light" or "ray" that will illuminate the target data while darkening the background. Referred to as "Laser Focus" the student will activate its power and control it like a gun, pointing it toward the target, firing and beaming its potent light. The imager will allow a creative visual to develop as the Laser Focus is maintained on the target. The same laser focus image should be used on each data unit. Remember, personalize the laser, allow it to focus and illuminate the data in whatever creative manner the imagination provides.

GUIDED IMAGERY EXERCISE INSTRUCTIONS:
— Find a comfortable position ... relax ... and begin focusing on your breathing.
— Let all your thoughts ... go ...
— Clear your mind.
— Activate your concentration energy system. P = 15 sec.
— You are now ready to begin.
— Take a moment now and begin activation of your "Laser Focus" P = 15 sec.
— It is now energized and ready to use.
— Bring your first data unit into view P = 5 sec.
— Now direct your laser and creatively see your data P = 10 sec.
— Alright ... stop ... and relax P = 10 sec.
— See your next data unit ... P = 5 sec.
— Laser focus P = 10 sec.
— Stop and relax P = 10 sec.
— Data unit P = 5 sec.
— Laser focus P = 10 sec.
— Stop and relax P = 10 sec.
— Data unit P = 5 sec.
— Laser focus P = 10 sec.
— Stop and relax P = 10 sec.
— Data unit P = 5 sec.
— Laser focus P = 10 sec.

— Stop and relax P = 10 sec.

[NOTE: Continue with this sequence if you like—don't exceed 15 data units.]

— Alright ... you have completed your laser focusing.
— Your data are now permanently filed in your memory system.
— Begin focusing on images of your original setting.
— When I count to five you will be back and alert.
— One-two-three-four-five.

NON-GUIDED IMAGERY EXERCISE INSTRUCTIONS:

Have the students select their target data. Explain what "Laser Focus" is and allow them to create an image for the technique. Encourage creativity. Instruct them on the length of time to be used for imaging each data unit, length of projection time for laser focus and how much time should be spent focusing on their data. Give an approximate length of time for the exercise. Experimenting with different types of laser focus images is great. However, should a student desire to use one particular image throughout the exercise, that is acceptable, too. Make sure the data are pre-determined. Students should have at least one type of laser focus image prior to beginning the exercise.

VARIATIONS:

A) Have the students create a different name for the laser focusing process.
B) Do repeated laser focus images for each data unit.
C) Provide specific dimensions for the creation of the laser, e.g., its beaming size, specific type of illumination, color, magnification process, etc.
D) Create guided image for developing a laser focus.
E) Provide a specific location, background where the laser focus can be used for memorizing the data.

FOLLOW-UP ACTIVITIES:

A) Have the students describe in detail their laser focus.
B) Create a drawing showing how the laser focus embellishes the data unit.
C) Make a list of other ways the laser focus can be used.
D) Write about the most interesting aspect of the laser focus technique.

MEMORY EXERCISE:
IMAGE REPETITION

MEMORY TECHNIQUE DESCRIPTION:
This exercise is based on repeated images of target data. Each data unit should be imaged for a duration of five seconds and then repeated three times in succession. There should be a ten second pause between data units. The imager may use any method for projecting his or her data, e.g., s/he may use a sign, a screen, a familiar setting, a color, etc. The key is to repeat the same image at least three times. Have the students pre-arrange target data.

GUIDED IMAGERY EXERCISE INSTRUCTIONS:
— Find comfortable position ... relax ... and begin focusing on your breathing ...
— Let all of your thoughts ... go ...
— Clear your mind ...
— Activate your concentration energy system P = 15 sec.
— You are now ready to begin.
— Fade-in data unit one ... P = 5 sec.
— Fade-out and relax ... P = 10 sec.
— Fade-in data unit one ... P = 5 sec.
— Fade-out and relax ... P = 10 sec.
— Fade-in data unit one ... P = 5 sec.
— Fade-out and relax ... P = 10 sec.
— Fade-in data unit two ... P = 5 sec.
— Fade-out and relax ... P = 10 sec.
— Fade-in data unit two ... P = 5 sec.
— Fade-out and relax ... P = 10 sec.
— Fade-in data unit two ... P = 5 sec.
— Fade-out and relax ... P = 10 sec.
[NOTE: Continue this procedure fading data in and out using the five and ten second pause for as many data units as you like. (Don't exceed 15 data units)]
— Alright ... you have completed your image repetitions.
— Your data are now permanently filed in your memory system.
— Begin focusing on images of your original setting.
— When I count to five you will be back and alert.
— One-two-three-four-five.

NON-GUIDED IMAGERY EXERCISE INSTRUCTIONS:

Explain the procedure for doing repeated images. Specify the duration of image projection (length of time for concentrating on image) and the exact number of repetitions. Have students pre-arrange their target data. Instruct students to relax after data are faded out. Provide a time structure for completing the exercise.

VARIATIONS:

A) Use different image projection and pausing times.
B) Use more or fewer image repetitions.
C) Allow the students to control the image projections.
D) Use multi-colors for each data unit.
E) Select a common setting or background for image projections.

FOLLOW-UP ACTIVITIES:

A) Make additional target data lists.
B) Describe how the images changed from one repetition to another.
C) Make a list of different backgrounds that could be used for image projection.
D) Describe how repetition one was different from repetition three with a particular data unit.

MEMORY EXERCISE:
SKY WRITING

MEMORY TECHNIQUE DESCRIPTION:
In this exercise the students are to select a particular method for writing their target data in the sky. An out-of-doors setting will be established for the exercise, e.g., a park on a beautiful day, or the top of a mountain, or lying on a beach on a warm sunny day. Prior to starting the sky writing students should take a few moments and image their setting as well as their sky writing method. Once this is accomplished, the guided image can begin. The imager will be instructed to write creatively in the sky each data unit pausing at appropriate times.

GUIDED IMAGERY EXERCISE INSTRUCTIONS:
— Find a comfortable position ... relax ... and begin focusing on your breathing ...
— Let all of your thoughts ... go ...
— Clear your mind.
— Activate your concentration energy system P = 15 sec.
— You are now ready to begin.
— You are now in a beautiful out-of-doors setting, relaxed and focused ... P = 5 sec.
— Take a moment and sense your surroundings ... P = 15 sec.
— You have already created a special sky writing method.
— Practice one time ... using your first name as a data unit.
— Begin now writing your first data unit in the sky.
— See it clearly ... P = 10 sec.
— Alright ... begin writing data unit two ... P = 10 sec.
— Data unit # 3 ... P = 10 sec.
— Data unit # 4 ... P = 10 sec.
— Data unit # 5 ... P = 10 sec.
— Data unit # 6 ... P = 10 sec.
[Continue through ten data units.]
— Alright ... you have completed your sky writing.
— Your data are now permanently filed in your memory system.
— Begin focusing on images of your original setting.
— When I count to five you will be back and alert.
— One-two-three-four-five.

NON-GUIDED IMAGERY EXERCISE INSTRUCTIONS:

Discuss the nature of sky writing allowing each student to develop a specific method. Use an out-of-doors setting for the exercise. Any method of sky writing is fine. Be sure students have pre-arranged their target data. Give them a time for each image projection and an approximate time for the exercise. Tell the students to relax in between data units.

VARIATIONS:
A) Select one method of sky writing and use for the entire group.
B) Have the students create images from two different perspectives, e.g., seeing the sky writing from the ground and then seeing it from within, an internal sensory perspective.
C) Use different sky writing methods for each data unit.
D) Do multiple repetitions of each data unit.
E) Use different writing speeds, e.g., high speed, super slow motion.

FOLLOW-UP ACTIVITIES:
A) Describe in detail your exact sky writing method.
B) Make a list of all the different ways of doing sky writing.
C) Write an advertisement announcing a new sky writing business.
D) Illustrate your sky writing method on a large sheet of paper.

MEMORY EXERCISE:
TEXTURES

MEMORY TECHNIQUE DESCRIPTION:
In this exercise the students are to use a variety of textures in their images. Each data unit presented will be experienced through a different texture. The data unit will not only be seen in the texture but will be felt and handled in any way the imager decides. The students should have a few textures in mind prior to beginning the exercise. Other textures needed as the data are displayed can be created at that moment. This will allow the student an opportunity to be spontaneous in his/her creation of data unit and texture. Pre-arrange data and follow suggested pausing signals. Be sure to provide the student sufficient time to experience data in a sensory manner.

GUIDED IMAGERY EXERCISE INSTRUCTIONS:
— Find a comfortable position ... relax and ... begin focusing on your breathing ...
— Let all of your thoughts ... go ...
— Clear your mind.
— Activate your concentration energy system ... P = 15 sec.
— You are now ready to begin.
— You are now going to experience each of your selected data units in a different texture.
— Once you have your image begin FEELING your data unit.
— Alright ... now let us begin with your data ...
— Data unit # 1 ... see it and feel its texture ... P = 15 sec.
— Fade-out and relax ... P = 5 sec.
— Data unit # 2 ... see it and feel its texture ... P = 15 sec.
— Fade-out and relax ... P = 5 sec.
— Data unit #3 ... see it and feel its texture ... P = 15 sec.
— Fade-out and relax ... P = 5 sec.
— Data unit # 4 ... see it and feel its texture ... P = 15 sec.
— Fade-out and relax ... P = 5 sec.
— Data unit # 5 ... see it and feel its texture ... P = 15 sec.
— Fade-out and relax ... P = 5 sec.
[NOTE: Continue sequence for more data.]

— Alright ... you have completed your texture images.
— Your data are now permanently filed in your memory system.
— Begin focusing on images of your original setting.
— When I count to five you will be back and alert.
— One-two-three-four-five.

NON-GUIDED IMAGERY EXERCISE INSTRUCTIONS:

Describe to students how the texture images will be experienced during image projection. Explain that they will have sufficient time to see and feel each data unit constructed according to an imagined texture. The textures should be different for each data unit. Provide an approximate time for image projection and fade-out. Have students develop a few texture ideas prior to beginning the exercise. Let the other texture ideas just come from their imaginations.

VARIATIONS:
A) Use one type of texture for all data.
B) Use guided instructions for seeing color of texture, shape, or other characteristics that you might think of that are appropriate.
C) Provide guided instructions on the type of texture to be used with each data unit, e.g., soft, hard, rough, etc.
D) Allow the student more time to experience the texture image and let them decide when to fade-out and relax.

FOLLOW-UP ACTIVITIES:
A) Describe each of your creative textures.
B) Give each texture image a name.
C) Describe the process of feeling your textured data unit.
D) Design a mural displaying all your textures.

MEMORY EXERCISE:
SOUNDS

MEMORY TECHNIQUE DESCRIPTION:
After selecting the target data, students will be guided through an imagery experience where they will have to create special sounds for each of their data units. The sounds will be different for each data unit. The students will be instructed to concentrate on their data and then allow a sound to come into their awareness. This sound will be associated with the data unit being projected. Students will have a designated time for focusing on the data, allowing the sound to emerge and to fade-out image and relax. Data should be pre-arranged.

GUIDED IMAGERY EXERCISE INSTRUCTIONS:
— Find a comfortable position ... relax ... and begin focusing on your breathing.
— Let all of your thoughts ... go ...
— Clear your mind.
— Activate your concentration energy system ... P = 15 sec.
— You are now ready to begin.
— You will concentrate on your data unit and then listen for your associated sound created from your imagination.
— Alright ... Focus on data unit # 1 ... P = 5 sec.
— Now listen to its sound ... P = 10 sec.
— Fade-out and relax ... P = 10 sec.
— Focus on data unit # 2 ... P = 5 sec.
— Listen to its sound ... P = 10 sec.
— Fade-out and relax ... P = 10 sec.
— Focus on data unit # 3 ... P = 5 sec.
— Listen to its sound ... P = 10 sec.
— Fade-out and relax ... P = 10 sec.
— Focus on data unit # 4 ... P = 5 sec.
— Listen to its sound ... P = 10 sec.
— Fade-out and relax ... P = 10 sec.
— Focus on data unit # 5 ... P = 5 sec.
— Listen to its sound ... P = 10 sec.
— Fade-out and relax ... P = 10 sec.

[NOTE: Continue sequence for more data.]
— Alright ... you have completed your images and sounds.
— Your data are now permanently filed in your memory system.
— Begin focusing on images of your original setting.
— When I count to five you will be back and alert.
— One-two-three-four-five.

NON-GUIDED IMAGERY EXERCISE INSTRUCTIONS:

Give the students an opportunity to pre-select their data and then to develop a few sounds that they might use for the exercise. Instruct the students that they must allow the sound being associated with the data unit just to float into their awareness. Be creative with the sound images and try to create different sounds for each data unit. Give them a time sequence for concentrating on their data and for listening to their sounds.

VARIATIONS:
A) Use one sound for more than one data unit.
B) Use other sensory cues, e.g., color, texture, etc.
C) Use one sound with several variations in pitch, tone, volume and intensity.
D) Provide the students with pre-recorded sounds as you guide them through the exercise.

FOLLOW-UP ACTIVITIES:
A) Make a data list with corresponding sounds.
B) Describe your most unusual sound.
C) Make a master list describing all of the sounds created by the class during the exercise. Categorize them.
D) Make a list of the various instruments heard during the exercise and other sources where the sounds may have originated.

MEMORY EXERCISE:
SCULPTURING

MEMORY TECHNIQUE DESCRIPTION:
In this exercise students will take their data units and sculpture them. They will actually see themselves using a substance to creatively sculpture their data. They may use any substance of their choice and any color or texture they like. The same material or substance should be used with all data in this exercise. Time must be provided for allowing the sculpture to be completed prior to moving on to the next data unit. A sequence will be used in the guided image. Encourage creativity in the style and shape of the sculpturing. Tell the students to feel the texture of their substance as they shape each individual data unit. The sculpturing should be completed in the same location, under the same conditions for the entire exercise. These conditions could change in future exercises.

GUIDED IMAGERY EXERCISE INSTRUCTIONS:
— Find a comfortable position ... relax ... and begin focusing on your breathing.
— Let all of your thoughts ... go ...
— Clear your mind.
— Activate your concentration energy system ... P = 15 sec.
— You are now ready to begin.
— Take a moment now and begin to play with your special sculpturing substance ... feel its texture ... P = 30 sec.
— Alright ... begin sculpturing your first data unit ... P = 30 sec.
— Fade-out and relax ... P = 10 sec.
— Begin sculpturing data unit # 2 ... P = 30 sec.
— Fade-out and relax ... P = 10 sec.
— Begin sculpturing data unit # 3 ... P = 30 sec.
— Fade-out and relax ... P = 10 sec.
— Begin sculpturing data unit # 4 ... P = 30 sec.
— Fade-out and relax ... P = 10 sec.
— Begin sculpturing data unit # 5 ... P = 30 sec.
— Fade-out and relax ... P = 10 sec.
[NOTE: Continue sequence for more data.]
— Alright ... you have completed sculpturing your data.
— Take a moment now and see all that you have sculptured ... P = 15 sec.

— You are now finished with this imagery exercise.
— Your data are now permanently filed in your memory system.
— Begin focusing on images of your original setting.
— When I count to five you will be back and alert.
— One-two-three-four-five.

NON-GUIDED IMAGERY EXERCISE INSTRUCTIONS:

Discuss the nature of the art of sculpturing. Tell the students that they will actually see themselves involved in this creative process. Ask the students to decide on a substance that they can use for sculpturing. They will use the same substance for each of their data units. Provide them with a time sequence for each data unit sculpture. When they finish one they should bring up a new data unit and begin sculpturing it. Have them be creative with their designs, take their time and totally feel and sense these creative manipulations.

VARIATIONS:
A) Give the students the type of substance to be used for sculpturing.
B) Use different colors for each sculptured data unit.
C) Paint each completed sculpture.
D) Use more sensory-type suggestions during the guided image, e.g., smell the sculpture, feel its texture, etc.

FOLLOW-UP ACTIVITIES:
A) Draw one or more of your completed sculptures.
B) Describe how you felt during the sculpturing process.
C) Which data unit provided you with the most unusual experience. Explain.
D) Describe your specific substance used in sculpturing.

MEMORY EXERCISE:
COLOR

MEMORY TECHNIQUE DESCRIPTION:
In this exercise the student will use a variety of colors for image projection. Each data unit will be imaged in a new and different color. The imager will first focus on the data then apply the color. Concentration on the colored data unit will last for approximately ten seconds then there will be a brief pause and relaxation. The imager may create any graphic or design for projecting his/her data unit. The image can have any background or setting that interests the student. Data should be pre-selected. The colors can be applied in a spontaneous random manner letting the imagination decide which color at what moment.

GUIDED IMAGERY EXERCISE INSTRUCTIONS:
— Find a comfortable position ... relax ... and begin focusing on your breathing.
— Let all of your thoughts ... go ...
— Clear your mind.
— Activate your concentration energy system ... P = 15 sec.
— You are now ready to begin.
— Image data unit # 1 ... P = 3 sec. ... NOW see it in color ... P = 15 sec.
— Fade-out and relax ... P = 10 sec.
— Image data unit # 2 ... P = 3 sec. ... NOW see it in color ... P = 15 sec.
— Fade-out and relax ... P = 10 sec.
— Image data unit # 3 ... P = 3 sec. ... NOW see it in color ... P = 15 sec.
— Fade-out and relax ... P = 10 sec.
— Image data unit # 4 ... P = 3 sec. ... NOW see it in color ... P = 15 sec.
— Fade-out and relax ... P = 10 sec.
— Image data unit # 5 ... P = 3 sec. NOW see it in color ... P = 15 sec.
— Fade-out and relax ... P = 10 sec.
— Image data unit # 6 ... P = 3 sec. NOW see it in color ... P = 15 sec.
— Fade-out and relax ... P = 10 sec.
— Image data unit # 7 ... P = 3 sec. NOW see it in color ... P — 15 sec.
— Fade-out and relax ... P = 10 sec.
[NOTE: Continue sequence for more data.]
— Alright ... you have completed your color images ...

— Your data are now permanently filed in your memory system.
— Begin focusing on images of your original setting.
— When I count to five you will be back and alert.
— One-two-three-four-five.

NON-GUIDED IMAGERY EXERCISE INSTRUCTIONS:
Have the students pre-select their data. Tell them that they will first project an image of their data unit, then they are to apply color to the image. They should maintain focus on the colored data unit for 10 seconds then just allow the image to fade-out. Their minds should then be cleared and ready for the next data unit projection. Repeat the procedure for several data units making sure that each data unit has a different color. Give them a time line for the exercise.

VARIATIONS:
A) Use one color for all data units.
B) Use multi-colored images for each data unit.
C) Use two-toned colored images for each data unit.
D) Use different shades of one color for all the data units.

FOLLOW-UP ACTIVITIES:
A) Make a list of data units in whatever color they were imaged during the exercise.
B) Take one data unit that was especially colorful in its projection and illustrate it on a large piece of drawing paper-use appropriate color(s) for the drawing.
C) Make a mural of all the data units seen in color.
D) Write about "My Most Unusual Color."

MEMORY EXERCISE:
SUPERLEARNING

MEMORY TECHNIQUE DESCRIPTION:
This is a special method that was developed by Dr. Geogi Lozanov of Sofia, Bulgaria. The method has been described in detail in a book written by Sheila Ostrander and Lynn Schroeder. Two major aspects of Superlearning make the approach unique and most effective. One is the use of a special type of Baroque music with a tempo of 60-70 beats per minute. Dr. Lozanov claims that this type of music has a very positive effect on one's central nervous system. He found that this slow movement of Baroque music relaxes the body while the mind becomes more alert (a special listing of Baroque music can be found in Appendix B). The other dimension of Superlearning is the pacing of spoken data. Lozanov discovered that an eight-second cycle for pacing spoken data was most effective and conducive for learning. The eight-second cycle has two bars of four beats or two frames of four seconds. During the first four beats of the cycle you remain silent. During the next four beats the data are said. A twelve beat cycle has also been used with success where there were more data to be presented. You are to hold your breath while the data is being said (either by another person or on a tape recorder).

Different intonations are recommended for each cycle.

NOTE: This exercise requires some preliminary work with the Baroque music and the pacing of data. Follow these steps:

Step 1   Discuss the method with your students.
Step 2   Have your students listen to several Baroque selections.
Step 3   Clearly outline the 8 and 12 second cycles, e.g., 8 sec. cycle — — — — /— — — — (first frame you exhale and inhale . . . second frame you hold your breath while the spoken data are being said) 12 sec. cycle — — — — — — /— — — — — —

Note: The type of data will determine the best cycle to use, e.g., two word terms or short phrases will require you to use the longer 12 second cycle.

Step 4   Conduct short practice sessions using both types of cycles.
Step 5   Discuss the method and student reactions.
Step 6   Experiment with a short data list (5-10 units)

After you have done some preliminary work with Superlearning you may wish to do the following exercise.

Decide on which cycle you will be using for this exercise. Select the appropriate Baroque music (see Music List, Appendix B). Explain to the students that they will be listening to a very relaxing type of music while they hear their data units being spoken at a special pace. During the four or six second frame where the data are being heard, students will concentrate on the spoken data in whatever manner they choose, i.e., they can just listen, or they can create an image of the data or even an association image of the data. The key is to remain relaxed and attentive.

REMEMBER: First four seconds . . . you exhale and inhale
Second four seconds . . . you hold your breath and listen to spoken data
One—two—three—four / One—two—three—four
(exhale and inhale)   (hold breath & listen to spoken data unit)

GUIDED IMAGERY EXERCISE INSTRUCTIONS:

— Find a comfortable position . . . relax . . . and begin focusing on your breathing . . . P = 30 sec.
— Let all of your thoughts . . . go . . .
— Clear your mind.
— Activate your concentration energy system . . . P = 15 sec.
— You are now ready to begin.
START BAROQUE MUSIC. . . HERE . . . P = 15 sec.
— Let us first focus on our breathing pattern.
— Exhale . . . Inhale . . . Hold Your Breath (2-4 sec. frames)
— Again . . . Exhale . . . Inhale . . . Hold Your Breath . . .
— Exhale . . . Inhale . . . Hold Your Breath . . .
— Alright . . . you will continue this breathing pattern as you will now hear your data . . .
START DATA TAPE . . . HERE . . .
— P a u s e . . . data unit . . .
— P a u s e . . . data unit . . .
NOTE: At this point the music is still playing and the data are being heard by the students (every four or six seconds a data unit should be spoken). Beginning exercise, use 15 to 20 data units; advanced exercise, use up to fifty data units
STOP DATA and STOP MUSIC . . . HERE . . .
— Alright . . . you have completed this special Superlearning exercise.
— Your data are now permanently filed in your memory system.

— Begin focusing on images of your original setting.
— When I count to five you will be back and alert.
— One-two-three-four-five.

NOTE: This exercise is very good for memorizing a long list of terms or a vocabulary list.

NON-GUIDED IMAGERY EXERCISE INSTRUCTIONS:
This exercise should be done through a guided image first, then if students are interested they can follow the procedures described above. An audio cassette tape that the student can play privately can very easily be made for a Superlearning exercise. The data bytes can be recorded by the teacher or the student using the prescribed cycle. As the data are being put onto the tape the Baroque music could also be recorded.

VARIATIONS:
A) You can say the commands exhale/inhale orally or just pause during that four second cycle.
B) Use different selections of music for each new exercise.
C) Use one of the relaxation exercises in Chapter 2 prior to beginning the exercise.
D) Experiment with different cycles for presenting data.
E) Experiment with different voice inflections when presenting the spoken data.

FOLLOW-UP ACTIVITIES:
A) Describe how your mind responded to the spoken data.
B) Describe your reaction to the Baroque music.
C) Describe how this exercise might work using different types of music.
D) Make a list of the type of data that would be appropriate for this method of learning.

MEMORY EXERCISE:
SLIDE SHOW

MEMORY TECHNIQUE DESCRIPTION:
In this exercise the student will create an imaginary slide projector. The data units will be seen as color slides which will be controlled by a special switch. The student will press the switch and immediately focus on the projected data unit. Concentration will be kept on the slide until the command of "fade-out" is given. Then the imager will bring on the next data unit. The student should create a vivid image of what the slide projector looks like and the viewing screen where the images will be shown. The data unit slides may be seen in any color or combination of colors that appeals to the imager. A familiar or an attractive setting should be created for the exercise.

GUIDED IMAGERY EXERCISE INSTRUCTIONS:
— Find a comfortable position ... relax ... and begin focusing on your breathing.
— Let all of your thoughts ... go ...
— Clear your mind.
— Activate your concentration energy system.
— You are now ready to begin.
— Begin by seeing yourself in a familiar room ... P = 10 sec.
— Next ... see a fully automatic color slide projector ... P = 10 sec.
— Observe a large viewing screen ... P = 10 sec.
— Now grab hold of a special control switch ... that will enable you to project colorful slides onto the screen ... P = 10 sec.
— Alright ... you are now ready to sit comfortably, relax ... and begin projecting your data units ...
— Data unit ... # 1 ... PROJECT ... P = 10 sec.
— Fade-out and relax ... P = 5 sec.
— Data unit ... # 2 ... PROJECT ... P = 10 sec.
— Fade-out and relax ... P = 5 sec.
— Data unit ... # 3 ... PROJECT ... P = 10 sec.
— Fade-out and relax ... P = 5 sec.
— Data unit ... # 4 ... PROJECT ... P = 10 sec.
— Fade-out and relax ... P = 5 sec.
— Data unit ... # 5 ... PROJECT ... P = 10 sec.

— Fade-out and relax ... P = 5 sec.
[NOTE: Continue sequence for more data.]
— Alright ... turn off your projector ... P = 5 sec.
— You have completed your special slide show ...
— Your data are now permanently filed in your memory system.
— Begin focusing on images of your original setting.
— When I count to five you will be back and alert.
— One-two-three-four-five.

NON-GUIDED IMAGERY EXERCISE INSTRUCTIONS:
Explain to the students exactly what a slide projector is and how it's operated. Discuss the procedure for projecting their data units in color onto a large screen. First have the students create images for a viewing room, a slide projector, and a large screen. Once these images are set the student can proceed with data projection. Provide structure for viewing and pausing times and indicate the approximate length of the exercise.

VARIATIONS:
A) Change the type of projector, e.g., make it an overhead projector, movie projector, etc.
B) Add special features to the color slides, e.g., use nature scenes as background, or abstract drawings.
C) Add sound to the slides. Have a voice saying each data unit or have music with each projection.
D) Use more detail in the guided image, e.g., have the students actually load each data unit slide into the projector, or write an ID number on each slide.
E) Project data unit slide for long time periods or perhaps run through the slides twice.

FOLLOW-UP ACTIVITIES:
A) Describe your viewing room, special automatic projector and large viewing screen.
B) Discuss how you can make this exercise different.
C) Describe how your data images appeared in slide format.
D) Tell about your strangest slide.

MEMORY EXERCISE:
MEMORY MONSTER

MEMORY TECHNIQUE DESCRIPTION:
In this exercise the students are to create an imaginary monster who has great power for memorizing data. The monster should be an original creation. Once the monster has been created the students then need to develop a means for giving the data to the monster. This process should be highly personalized and imaginative. In the guided image exercise the student will have to create a method for presenting the data units to the monster. The monster will be brought onto the scene and will be ready to accommodate the students' orders. The student is to give all the data units to the monster in some self-selected manner. Encourage creativity and do the exercise slowly, pausing so that the imager has time to develop clarity and vividness in his/her images.

GUIDED IMAGERY EXERCISE INSTRUCTIONS:
— Find a comfortable position ... relax ... and begin focusing on your breathing.
— Let all of your thoughts ... go ...
— Clear your mind.
— Activate your concentration energy system ... P = 15 sec.
— You are now ready to begin.
— With your imagination I want you to now create your own memory monster ... P = 30 sec.
— This new creature has extraordinary power for memorizing data.
— In a moment you will give your data to your monster ...
— Now create a setting in which you can clearly see your monster ready for assignment ... P = 10 sec.
— Alright ... in a very creative way I want you to present your data units to your monster ...
— Make the data available ... and allow the monster to put these data into his/her incredible memory system ...
— Alright...begin giving the monster your data units ... P = 1 min.
— Your monster now has all your data ... they are locked in his/her powerful memory system.

— You are only to ask ... and your monster will deliver any or all of your data.
— Say good-bye to your monster ... P = 15 sec.
— Alright ... you have completed this exercise.
— Your data are now permanently filed in your memory system.
— Begin focusing on images of your original setting.
— When I count to five you will be back and alert.
— One-two-three-four-five.

NON-GUIDED IMAGERY EXERCISE INSTRUCTIONS:
Have the students create their memory monster and a special creative process for having the monster receive their data. They can present the data in whatever manner they like and as many data units as their monster can handle. Tell them to be creative and give them plenty of time for developing the monster and for the memorization process.

VARIATIONS:
A) Provide the students with special features to include in the monster creation.
B) Present each data unit separately to the monster.
C) Create a common setting where the monster can be found.
D) Have the monster do other things especially relating to thinking and learning.
E) Provide a special method that the monster can use in memorizing your data.

FOLLOW-UP ACTIVITIES:
A) Tell why your "Memory Monster" is so fantastic.
B) Draw a picture illustrating the exact process your monster uses for memorizing data.
C) Make a list of all the amazing things your monster can do to help students learn.
D) Write a story about the relationship you are going to have with your memory monster.

MEMORY EXERCISE:
WET SAND

MEMORY TECHNIQUE DESCRIPTION:

This exercise is a multi-sensory experience where the students will see and feel themselves writing their data in wet sand along the sea shore. The setting will be established first, then the imager can proceed with writing the data. Have the students think about their favorite sea shore and a particular time of year and characteristics of a certain type of day. Once this is conceptualized the imagery experience can begin. During guided imagery, allow enough time for the students to get comfortably into the theme and setting. Use appropriate descriptors for emphasizing the climate and environmental conditions.

GUIDED IMAGERY EXERCISE INSTRUCTIONS:
— Find a comfortable position ... relax ... and begin focusing on your breathing.
— Let all of your thoughts ... go ...
— Clear your mind.
— Activate your concentration energy system ... P = 15 sec.
— You are now ready to begin.
— You are standing on the sandy beach of a beautiful ocean resort on a magnificent day ... P = 15 sec.
— You feel the sand under your feet and between your toes ...
— You smell the ocean air ... and feel a gentle breeze blowing against your face ... P = 15 sec.
— You feel relaxed and peaceful ...
— Take a moment now ... and sense your surroundings ... P = 30 sec.
— Alright ... I want you to clearly see an area where there is smooth wet sand ... where the ocean wave gently runs up and over the sand ... P = 15 sec.
— As the wave subsides and runs back into the sea you are going to write your data with your finger ... you are going to feel the wetness and texture of the sand.
— Alright ... let's begin ...
— Wave running up ... wave running back down ... smoothness ...
— Write data unit ... see it and feel it ... P = 10 sec.
— Wave running up ... wave running back down ... smoothness ...

— Write data unit ... see it and feel it ... P = 10 sec.
— Wave running up ... wave running back down ... smoothness...
— Write data unit ... see it and feel it ... P = 10 sec.
— Wave running up ... wave running back down ... smoothness ...
— Write data unit ... see it and feel it ... P = 10 sec.
— Wave running up ... wave running back down ... smoothness ...
[NOTE: Continue sequence for more data.]
— Alright ... you have finished writing your data ...
— Take a moment now and see this beautiful setting ... P = 10 sec.
— Your data are now permanently filed in your memory system.
— Begin focusing on images of your original setting.
— When I count to five you will be back and alert.
— One-two-three-four-five.

NON-GUIDED IMAGERY EXERCISE INSTRUCTIONS:

Explain the procedure for writing in wet sand. Have students establish a sea shore setting. Describe the process for having waves wash away each of the data units once they have been written in the sand. Have the students listen to the sounds of ocean waves (see Music List, Appendix B) as they do the exercise. Be sure the students give themselves enough time to create the sea shore setting prior to beginning writing their data. Have the student write as many data units in the sand as s/he would like.

VARIATIONS:

A) Use something other than a finger to write in the sand.
B) Take the students to a specific location.
C) Use appropriate ocean sounds or music to create a more sensory experience.
D) Use a camera and take a picture of each data unit written in the sand.

FOLLOW-UP ACTIVITIES:

A) Describe your sea shore setting. Be specific.
B) Describe your feeling as you were writing in the sand.
C) Describe the action of the waves as they run up and down the beach.
D) Draw, paint, sketch a picture of one of your data units written in the wet sand.

MEMORY EXERCISE:
BALLOON

MEMORY TECHNIQUE DESCRIPTION:
In this exercise the student will use a special marker to write his/her data onto an uninflated balloon. When the data unit is written on the balloon the student then inflates the balloon with helium and releases it up into the sky. The same procedure is used for each data unit. The student may use different colored markers or balloons as long as the data can be easily read. The balloons may be inflated to any size by any method. Data should be concentrated on as the balloon lifts into the air. Soft New Age music would be a plus for this exercise.

GUIDED IMAGERY EXERCISE INSTRUCTIONS:
— Find a comfortable position . . . relax . . . and begin focusing on your breathing.
— Let all of your thoughts . . . go . . .
— Clear your mind.
— Activate your concentration energy system . . . P = 15 sec.
— You are now ready to begin.
— You're in an outdoor area on a beautiful day
START MUSIC
— You have lots of magic markers and balloons.
— You are going to write your data unit on your balloon, fill it with helium, knot it, and let it float gently into the sky.
— Alright . . . write data unit # 1 . . . P = 10 sec.
— Fill your balloon with helium . . . P = 5 sec.
— See your enlarged data unit as the balloon floats up . . . up P = 10 sec.
— Write data unit # 2 . . . P = 10 sec.
— Fill your balloon . . . P = 5 sec.
— Watch the balloon float away . . . P = 10 sec.
— Write data unit # 3 . . . P = 10 sec.
— Fill your balloon . . . P = 5 sec.
— Watch the balloon float away . . . P = 10 sec.
— Write data unit # 4 . . . P = '0 sec.
— Fill your balloon . . . P = 5 sec.
— Watch the balloon float away . . . P = 10 sec.
— Write data unit # 5 . . . P = 10 sec.

— Fill your balloon ... P = 5 sec.
— Watch the balloon float away ... P = 10 sec.
[NOTE: Continue sequence for more data.]
— Alright ... you have completed the exercise.
— Your data are now permanently filed in your memory system.
— Begin focusing on images of your original setting.
— When I count to five you will be back and alert.
— One-two-three-four-five.

NON-GUIDED IMAGERY EXERCISE INSTRUCTIONS:
Describe the procedure for writing on the inflated balloon. After the student writes his/her data onto the balloon explain how they will fill the balloon with helium, knot it and let it float up into the sky. Tell the students that they may use any color markers and any size balloons.

Be sure to give them guidelines for image projection and pausing times. Let the students first become familiar with the outdoor setting prior to beginning the exercise. Have them concentrate on the data as the balloon lifts upward.

VARIATIONS:
A) Use one type of writing device and/or balloon.
B) Write one data unit on several different shaped balloons.
C) Have the exercise take place in a pre-determined location.
D) Add creative features to your balloon, e.g., a logo, decorations, music, movement, etc.

FOLLOW-UP ACTIVITIES:
A) Illustrate how your data unit appeared on the balloon.
B) Make a large drawing of all your balloons floating in the sky.
C) Tell about your most exciting balloon.
D) Describe the location used for your balloon experience.
E) Make a list of all the different things you could do with your balloon.

MEMORY EXERCISE:
PRINTSHOP

MEMORY TECHNIQUE DESCRIPTION:
The students will use a familiar computer for this exercise. They will type their data into a computer program called, "Printshop." Once the data units are typed into the program, the computer will then display the data on large banners. The imager will see his/her data typed on the banner then displayed on a familiar wall in some designated room. The students may use any type style and any type of printer. Concentration should be directed toward the computer monitor as the data units are being typed and as the data units are being printed onto the large banner. Use a high speed printer and a colored monitor. Change the type style for each data unit.

GUIDED IMAGERY EXERCISE INSTRUCTIONS:
— Find a comfortable position ... relax ... and begin focusing on your breathing.
— Let all of your thoughts ... go ...
— Clear your mind.
— Activate your concentration energy system ... P = 15 sec.
— You are now ready to begin.
— You are sitting in front of a computer.
— Notice the keyboard and the colored monitor.
— Your computer program is ready and waiting for data.
— First......type MEMORY: PRINTSHOP ... see it on your screen P = 10 sec.
— Type Data unit # 1 and see it on your screen ... P = 10 sec.
— Now tell your computer to print your data unit onto a large banner.
— See it being printed ... listen to the sounds ... P = 10 sec.
— Now take your banner and hang it in your room ... P = 10 sec.
— Type Data unit # 2 and see it on your screen ... P = 10 sec.
— Print data unit ... P = 10 sec.
— Display data in your room ... P = 10 sec.
— Type Data unit # 3 ... P = 10 sec.
— Print data unit ... P = 10 sec.
— Display data in your room ... P = 10 sec.
— Type Data unit # 4 ... P = 10 sec.

— Print data unit ... P = 10 sec.
— Display data in your room ... P = 10 sec.
— Type Data unit # 5 ... P = 10 sec.
— Print data unit ... P = 10 sec.
— Display data in your room ... P = 10 sec.
[NOTE: Continue sequence for more data.]
— Alright ... you have finished with the Printshop Program.
— Turn off your computer.
— Your data are now permanently filed in your memory system.
— Begin focusing on images of your original setting.
— When I count to five you will be back and alert.
— One-two-three-four-five.

NON-GUIDED IMAGERY EXERCISE INSTRUCTIONS:
Instead of guiding the students through the process of Type-Print-Display, each student will use a self-selected program for imaging their data. Tell them to follow the Type-Print-Display procedure, but perform it in any manner they like. Specify the time allotted for the exercise and encourage the students to use diversified type style and print format for their work. Pause between image projections and don't exceed 10-15 data units.

VARIATIONS:
A) Designate the type and style of computer ... and include more specific guided instructions for running the Printshop program.
B) Take one data unit and print it in several type styles.
C) Use specific colors for both typing and printing.
D) Have computer speak out each letter of data unit as it is being typed onto the monitor screen.

FOLLOW-UP ACTIVITIES:
A) Draw a picture of your computer and printer ... giving it a special name.
B) Illustrate the different type styles used in printing out the data units.
C) Write a special program for "Printshop," e.g., specific commands, special functions or some even amazing features.
D) Make a list of other types of memory exercises that your computer can produce.

MEMORY EXERCISE:
MURAL

MEMORY TECHNIQUE DESCRIPTION:
The students will select a setting where they can take their data units and draw them in the form of a large mural. A large sheet of paper or board will be needed. Different colors of paint should be used in the drawings. Students can arrange the painted data units in whatever shape or pattern they like. The mural should be framed and placed in an appropriate setting. The different senses should be emphasized during the guided image, e.g., feel the brush, smell the paint, etc.

GUIDED IMAGERY EXERCISE INSTRUCTIONS:
— Find a comfortable position . . . relax . . . and begin focusing on your breathing.
— Let all of your thoughts . . . go . . .
— Clear your mind.
— Activate your concentration energy system . . . P = 15 sec.
— You are now ready to begin.
— See yourself in a comfortable room ready to paint a great big mural . . . P = 10 sec.
— See your mural board and the many different colors of paint.
— Observe the different size paint brushes . . . P = 15 sec.
— Alright . . . begin your mural, painting each of your data units in whatever way you like.
— Data unit # 1 . . . PAINT . . . P = 15 sec.
— Fade-out and relax . . . P = 10 sec.
— Data unit # 2 . . . PAINT . . . P = 15 sec.
— Fade-out and relax . . . P = 10 sec.
— Data unit # 3 . . . PAINT . . . P = 15 sec.
— Fade-out and relax . . . P = 10 sec.
— Data unit # 4 . . . PAINT . . . P = 15 sec.
— Fade-out and relax . . . P = 10 sec.
— Data unit # 5 . . . PAINT . . . P = 15 sec.
— Fade-out and relax . . . P = 10 sec.
— Data unit # 6 . . . PAINT . . . P = 15 sec.

— Fade-out and relax ... P = 10 sec.
[NOTE: Continue sequence for more data.]
— Alright ... you have completed your mural, take a moment now and see all your drawn data ... P = 30 sec.
— See your mural now in its designated setting ... P = 10 sec.
— Your data are now permanently filed in your memory system.
— Begin focusing on images of your original setting.
— When I count to five you will be back and alert.
— One-two-three-four-five.

NON-GUIDED IMAGERY EXERCISE INSTRUCTIONS:
Instruct the students as to what a mural should be like and the materials necessary to create it. Explain that each data unit will be drawn on the mural using different colors. Tell the students to use different senses while concentrating on the data, e.g., feel, smell, etc. Give them an approximate time for completing the drawing. Be sure they take a moment and focus on the completed mural in some setting of their choice.

VARIATIONS:
A) Instead of painting use another art medium for completing the mural.
B) Designate the color to be used with each data unit.
C) Specify the setting where the mural should be painted, e.g., on a particular wall, ceiling, building, stage, etc.
D) Have the students paint the mural using their own time sequence for each data unit, i.e., their own fade-in and fade-out times.

FOLLOW-UP ACTIVITIES:
A) Actually paint the mural as was seen in the imaginary mural.
B) Describe how you felt while painting the mural.
C) Make a list of all the different ways a mural could be done.
D) Which form of imagery did you primarily use during the exercise? Internal or External Imagery? Explain.

MEMORY EXERCISE:
FINGER PAINTING

MEMORY TECHNIQUE DESCRIPTION:
In this exercise the students will draw their data units using finger paint. Each data unit will have its own color and will be displayed on a separate sheet of finger paint paper. When the drawings are complete the student will take a mental photograph of each one prior to ending the exercise. Emphasis should be on the sensory experience of feeling the paint as it glides along the shiny white paper. Background music would be very appropriate for this exercise as it is very conducive for relaxation.

GUIDED IMAGERY EXERCISE INSTRUCTIONS:
— Find a comfortable position ... relax ... and begin focusing on your breathing.
— Let all of your thoughts ... go ...
— Clear your mind.
— Activate your concentration energy system ... P = 15 sec.
— You are now ready to begin.
— Take a moment now ... and see all your material ...
— Paint ... paper ... comfortable setting ... P = 15 sec.
— Alright ... begin your finger painting with data unit # 1 ... P = 15 sec.
— Feel the texture as your fingers glide across the paper ... P = 10 sec.
— Fade-out and relax ... P = 10 sec.
— Data unit # 2 BEGIN FINGER PAINTING ... P = 15 sec.
— Fade-out and relax .... P = 10 sec.
— Data unit # 3 BEGIN FINGER PAINTING ... P = 15 sec.
— Fade-out and relax ... P = 10 sec.
— Data unit # 4 BEGIN FINGER PAINTING ... P = 15 sec.
— Fade-out and relax ... P = 10 sec.
— Data unit # 5 BEGIN FINGER PAINTING ... P = 15 sec.
— Fade-out and relax ... P = 10 sec.
[NOTE: Continue sequence for more data.]
— Alright ... you have completed your finger painting.
— Take a moment ... now ... and vividly see each of your finger paintings ... P = 30 sec.
— Let the images fade ...
— Your data are now permanently filed in your memory system.

— Begin focusing on images of your original setting.
— When I count to five you will be back and alert.
— One-two-three-four-five.

NON-GUIDED IMAGERY EXERCISE INSTRUCTIONS:
The students will finger paint each of their pre-selected data units according to their own time structure. They should use different colors and focus on the feeling sensations created through finger painting. Give them a time limit for the exercise and suggest the use of music as relaxing background.

VARIATIONS:
A) Put all the finger paintings onto one large sheet of paper or oak tag.
B) Use specific guided instructions for the finger movement.
C) Make a pre-recorded tape of different music selections to be played during each finger painting (they could be 30 to 60 sec. in duration, or longer if you like).
D) Let the imager fade-out of each drawing when ready.

FOLLOW-UP ACTIVITIES:
A) Illustrate one of your finger paint drawings.
B) Describe how the music influenced your movement in the drawing.
C) Write a guided image where students use their feet and toes instead of their fingers in the drawing.
D) Describe your favorite finger painting.

MEMORY EXERCISE:
SONGS

MEMORY TECHNIQUE DESCRIPTION:
The students will focus on their data units and then allow the sounds of a familiar song to come into their awareness. They will maintain concentration on the data unit as the song plays in their mind. When the song is finished the data unit will fade-out. After a brief relaxation the next data unit will fade-in and create the sounds of a new song. The sequence will be followed for no more than ten data units.

GUIDED IMAGERY EXERCISE INSTRUCTIONS:
— Find a comfortable position ... relax ... and begin focusing on your breathing.
— Let all of your thoughts ... go ...
— Clear your mind.
— Activate your concentration energy system ... P = 15 sec.
— You are now ready to begin.
— As you focus on your data you will hear the sounds of familiar songs ... just listen as the song plays ...
— Data unit # 1 ... LISTEN TO THE SONG ... P = 15 sec.
— Fade-out and relax ... P = 10 sec.
— Data unit # 2 ... LISTEN TO THE SONG ... P = 15 sec.
— Fade-out and relax ... P = 10 sec.
— Data unit #6 3 ... LISTEN TO THE SONG ... P = 15 sec.
Fade-out and relax ... P = 10 sec.
— Data unit # 4 ... LISTEN TO THE SONG ... P = 15 sec.
— Fade-out and relax ... P = 10 sec.
— Data unit # 5 ... LISTEN TO THE SONG ... P = 15 sec.
— Fade-out and relax ... P = 10 sec.
NOTE: Continue sequence for more data.
— Alright ... you have finished creating songs for your data.
— Your data are now permanently filed in your memory system.
— Begin focusing on images of your original setting.
— When I count to five you will be back and alert.
— One-two-three-four-five.

NON-GUIDED IMAGERY EXERCISE INSTRUCTIONS:
Explain to the students that they are to focus and concentrate on their data units and then allow the sounds of a familiar song to float into their awareness. As they continue to focus on the data they will just listen to the song play until a decision is made to fade-out the data unit. The data needs to be pre-selected, however, the songs can be created spontaneously during the experience. Provide a time structure and be sure the student pauses between data unit projections.

VARIATIONS:
A) Use a different type or style of music for each data unit.
B) Use one familiar song and allow the imager to project all the data units in the exercise in a continuous manner.
C) Pre-record several songs and use them during the guided image (use pauses in between songs).
D) Add other features, e.g., a specific location, create a video for the song and data unit, use nature images along with the song, have a color associated with each song.

FOLLOW-UP ACTIVITIES:
A) Make a data unit list with corresponding songs.
B) Describe your favorite image.
C) Make a list of other songs you might have used in this exercise.
D) Create an image experience where songs are used in a memory exercise.

MEMORY EXERCISE:
PHOTO ALBUM

MEMORY TECHNIQUE DESCRIPTION:

In this exercise the student will image each of his/her data units in an imagined "Photo Album." Each page of the album will contain another data unit. The album can be used for future exercises. The imager will slowly turn each page of the album and concentrate on the data unit. The album may be created and visualized in any format. The album can be used to store any data that the student may wish to remember. Become familiar with the album cover first, then begin the data projection.

GUIDED IMAGERY EXERCISE INSTRUCTIONS:
— Find a comfortable position ... relax ... and begin focusing on your breathing.
— Let all of your thoughts ... go ...
— Clear your mind.
— Activate your concentration energy system ... P = 15 sec.
— You are now ready to begin.
— You have obtained a special "Photo Album" ... take a moment now to see and feel this special possession ... P = 15 sec.
— Alright ... I want you to see the album in front of you now as you begin data unit projection.
— Open the album and see data unit # 1 ... P = 10 sec.
— Now go to the second page and see data unit # 2 ... P = 10 sec.
— Page three ... data unit # 3 ... P = 10 sec.
— Page four ... data unit # 4 ... P = 10 sec.
— Page five ... data unit # 5 ... P = 10 sec.
— Page six ... data unit # 6 ... P = 10 sec.
— Page seven ... data unit # 7 ... P = 10 sec.
NOTE: Continue sequence for more data.
— Alright ... close your album ... you have completed the exercise.
— Your data are now permanently filed in your memory system.
— Begin focusing on images of your original setting.
— When I count to five you will be back and alert.
— One-two-three-four-five.

NON-GUIDED IMAGERY EXERCISE INSTRUCTIONS:
Have the students create an imaginary "Photo Album" in which they will put their data. Each data unit should have its own page. Students should create images of their data as they slowly turn each page. At least ten seconds of image projection should be used with each page. Become familiar with the album and put it in a safe place. Ten to fifteen pages would seem to be appropriate for one exercise.

VARIATIONS:
A) Use some other type of book or document for storing data units.
B) Color code each page of the album.
C) Write the data unit onto the page of the album.
D) Slide the typed data unit into a clear pocket on each page.
E) Create a special setting where the album may be used, e.g., a favorite room, vacation spot, building, etc.

FOLLOW-UP ACTIVITIES:
A) Describe exactly what your album looks like.
B) Make a list of other things to put into the album.
C) How else could you design each of the album pages?
D) Describe your album three years from now!

CHAPTER 4 REFERENCES

BIBLIOGRAPHY
APPENDIX A

Ahsen, A. *Psyche: Self-analytic consciousness.* New York: Brandon House, 1977.

Atkinson, R.C. Mnemotechnics in second-language learning. *American Psychologist*, 30, 821-828, 1975.

Bagley, M.T. & Hess, K. *200 Ways of using imagery in the classroom.* New York: Trillium Press, 1984.

Bagley, M.T. *Using imagery in creative problem solving.* New York: Trillium Press, 1987.

Baldwin, B. *What you think is what you get.* Wilmington, North Carolina: Direction Dynamics, 1984.

Brown, B. *New mind-new body*. New York: Harper & Row Publishers, 1974.

Brown, B. *Supermind*. New York: Harper & Row Publishers, 1980.

Garfield, C. *Peak performance*. Palo Alto, CA: Performance Sciences, Inc., 1980.

Gawain, S. *Creative visualization*. New York: Bantam Books, 1978.

Gunther, B. *Sense relaxation*. New York: MacMillan, 1968.

Jacobsen, E. *You must relax*. New York: McGraw Hill, 1957.

Lorayne, H. & Lucas, J. *The memory book*. New York: Ballantine Books, 1974.

Lozanov, G. in *Superlearning*. Ostrander, S. & Schroder, L. New York: Dell Publishing Co., Inc., 1979.

Maltz, M. *Psycho-cybernetics*. New York: Pocket Books, 1963.

McKim, R. *Experience in visual thinking*. Belmont, CA: Wadsworth, 1972.

Ostrander, S. & Schroder, L. *Superlearning*. New York: Dell Publishing Co., Inc., 1979.

Paivio, A. *Imagery and verbal processes*. New York: Holt Rinehart & Winston, 1971.

Peale, N.V. *Positive imaging*. New York: Fawcett Crest, 1982.

Sheinen, K. *Mental imaging: Historical review, current application and educational implications*. Unpublished report, 1985.

APPENDIX B
NEW AGE MUSIC LIST

The Angels of Comfort (Side A), Angel Play (Side B). Inter-Dimensional Music, Box 594, Wald Pt., Sausalito, CA 94965

Bamboo Waterfall. Tape Masters, 176 Forest Ave., Pacific Grove, CA 93950

Spectrum Suite-Extended Play. Halpern Sounds, 1775 Old Country Rd. #9, Belmont, CA 94002

Music For An Inner Journey. Steve Bergman, P.O. Box 4577, Carmel, CA 93921

A Thousand Moods. Sona Gala Productions, 1845 N. Farwell Ave., Milwaukee, WI 53202

Golden Voyage. Awakening Productions, Inc. 4132 Tuller Ave., Culver City, CA 90230

Source Sampler, Vol. 1. Source Music, 1307 Buena Vista, Pacific Grove, CA 93950

The Atlantis Healing Harp. Valley of the Sun Publishing, Box 38, Malibu, CA 90265

Omni Suite (Mu-1) by Steven Bergman. Potential Unlimited, Inc. 4808-H Broadmoon S.E., Grand Rapids, MI 49508

Valley of the Birds (Mu-8) by Emerald Web. Potential Unlimited, Inc.

Nature's Paradise (Mu-7) by Sal Rachele. Potential Unlimited, Inc.

Morning Dance (Mu-17) by Dyveke Spino. Potential Unlimited, Inc.

Dawn (M-DN 432) by Steven Halpern. Institute of Human Development, P.O. Box 1616, Ojai, CA 93023

Slow Ocean (OCN), Institute of Human Development

Silk Road (M-SK 332) by Kitaro. Institute of Human Development

APPENDIX C
BAROQUE MUSIC LIST

Bach, J.S.
— Largo from Concerto in G Minor for Flute and Strings, BWV 1056 (2:53) Bach and Telemann Flute Concertos, Jean-Pierre Rampal, Saar Radio Chamber Orchestra, Odyssey-Columbia Records.

— Aria (or Sarabande) to The Goldberg Variations, BWV 988, Millicent Silver, harpsichord, Saga Records.

- Largo from Harpsicord Concerto in F Minor, BWV 1056 (2:40), Greatest Hits of 1720, Judith Norell, harpsicord, Philharmonia Virtuosi of New York, Columbia Records.

- Largo from Solo Harpsicord Concerto in G Minor, BWV 975, 6 Concerti after Vivaldi, Janos Sebestyen, harpsicord, Turnabout, Vox Records.

- Largo from Solo Harpsicord Concerto in C Major, BWV 976, 6 Concerti after Vivaldi, Janos Sebestyen, harpsicord, Turnabout, Vox Records.

- Largo from Solo Harpsicord Concerto in F Major, BWV 978

Corelli, A.
- Saranda (largo) from Concerto no. 7 in D Minor, 12 Concerti Grossi op. 5 (violin, cello, and harpsicord), Gli Accademici di Milano, Vox Records.

- Preludio (largo) and Sarabanda (largo) from Concerto no. 8 in E Minor, 12 Concerti Grossi, op. 5, Gli Accademici di Milano, Vox Records.

- Preludio (largo) from Concerto no. 9 in A Major; Sarabanda (largo) from Concerto no. 10 in F Major, both from 12 Concerti Grossi op. 5, Vox Records.

- From Corelli's Twelve Concerti Grossi, Opus 6, any of the largo movements can be used.

Handel, G.F.
- Largo from Concerto no.1 in F (brass) from Music for the Royal Fireworks London Symphony Orchestra, Angel Records.

- Largo from Concerto no. 3 in D (brass) from Music for the Royal Fireworks London Symphony Orchestra, Angel Records.

- Largo from Concerto no. 1 in B-flat Major, op. 3 (woodwinds and strings), Concerti Grossi, op. 3, Mainz Chamber Orchestra, Turnabout, Vox Records.

From Handel's Twelve Concerti Grossi, Opus 6, any of the largo movements can be used.

Telemann, G.
- Largo from Double Fantasia in G Major for Harpsicord, 6 Fantasias for Harpsicord, Leonard Hokanson, harpsicord, World Series; Philips.

- Largo from Concerto in G Major for Viola and String Orchestra, Wurttemberg Chamber Orchestra, Turnabout, Vox Records.

Vivaldi, A.

— Largo from "Winter" from The Four Seasons, Lola Bobesco, violin, The Heidelberg Chamber Orchestra, Peerless Records.

— Largo from Concerto in D Major for Guitar and Strings from Baroque Guitar Concerti, Konrad Ragossnig, guitar; and the Southwest German Chamber Orchestra, Turnabout, Vox Records.

— Largo from Concerto in C Major for Mandolin, Strings and Harpsicord, P. 134 (1:55)

— Largo from Concerto in D Minor for Viola D'Amore, Strings and Harpsicord, P.288 (2:15)

— Largo from Concerto in F Major for Viola D'Amore, Two Oboes, Bassoon, Two Horns and Figured Bass, P. 286 (4:27); Three Concertos for Viola D'Amore, Two Concertos for Mandolin, The New York Sinfonietta, Odyssey Records.

— Largo from Flute Concerto No. 4 in G Major, 6 Flute Concerti Opus 10 Jean-Pierre Rampal, flute, Louis de Froment Chamber Ensemble, Turnabout, Vox Records.

APPENDIX D
RESEARCH STUDIES ON IMAGERY-LEARNING-MEMORY

Bracken, B. Relative imagery-evoking ability of personalized and non-personalized sentences. *Journal of Mental Imagery*, 5, 121-124, 1981.

Gambrill, L.B. & Koskinen, P. Mental imagery and reading comprehension of below average readers: Paper presented at the annual meeting of the American Educational Research Assoc., March, 1982.

Goodwin, N. Dancing on the stage in your head. *English Journal*, 43-45, 1983.

Higbee, K. L. Recent research on visual mnemonics: Historical roots and educational fruits. *Review of Educational Research*, 49, 611-629, 1979.

Lesgold, A., McMormick, C. & Golingkoff, R. Imagery training and children's prose learning. *Journal of Educational Psychology*, 67, 663-667, 1975.

Montague, W.E. & Carter, J.F. Vividness of imagery recalling connected discourse. *Journal of Educational Psychology*, 64, 72-75, 1973.

Paivio, A. & Katz, A. Imagery variables in concept identification. *Journal of Verbal Learning and Verbal Behavior*, 14, 284-293, 1975.

Pressley, M. G. Mental imagery helps eight year-olds remember what they read. *Journal of Educational Psychology*, 68, 355-359, 1975.

Pressley, M. G., Levin, J. R. & Delaney, H. The mnemonic keyword method. *Review of Educational Research*, 52, 61-91, 1982.

Radaker, L. D. The effect of visual imagery spelling performance. *Journal of Educational Research*, 56, 370-372, 1963.

Rose, M., Cundick, B., & Higbee, K. Verbal rehearsal and visual memory: mnemonic aids for learning disabled children. *Journal of Learning Disabilities* 16, 352-354. 1983.

Vander Veur, B.W. Imagery ratings of 1,000 frequently used words. *Journal of Educational Psychology*, 67, 44-56, 1975.

IMAGERY NOTES

IMAGERY NOTES

IMAGERY NOTES

IMAGERY NOTES

IMAGERY NOTES

IMAGERY NOTES

IMAGERY NOTES

IMAGERY NOTES

IMAGERY NOTES